Managing God's Money
—The Basics

Become

A Good

Manager

Of God's

Resources

Managing God's Money
–*The Basics*

Michel A. Bell

Essence PUBLISHING

Belleville, Ontario, Canada

Managing God's Money—The Basics

Copyright © 2000, Michel A. Bell

ISBN: 1-55306-086-5

1st Printing, February 2000
2nd Printing, November 2001

Essence Publishing is a Christian Book Publisher dedicated to furthering the work of Christ through the written word. For more information, contact: 44 Moira Street West, Belleville, Ontario, Canada K8P 1S3.
Phone: 1-800-238-6376. Fax: (613) 962-3055.
E-mail: info@essencegroup.com
Internet: www.essencegroup.com
Printed in Canada
by

Essence
PUBLISHING

I dedicate this book to
my grandchildren,
Adrienne, Jesse and Dylan,
who in unison all shout,
"Twins"!!!

Essential Concepts

GAS Principle: Three Key Truths in the Bible concerning money:

- **Key Truth #1: God Owns Everything** (Psalm 24:1-2, Colossians 1:16)
- **Key Truth #2: Accept What You Have** (1 Timothy 6:7-8, Hebrews 13:5)
- **Key Truth #3: Seek First His Kingdom and Submit Your Requests to Him** (Matthew 6:33, Proverbs 19:21)

PEACE Budgetary Control System: A system that allows you to achieve **goals** systematically in the following manner:

- **PLAN** for a specific period to accomplish precise **goals**.
- **ESTIMATE** and record the expenses needed to achieve those **goals**.
- **ACT** on the **plan and record** actual results as you progress toward your **goals**.
- **COMPARE actual** results **with** the **plan** and with the **estimated expenses** required to attain the **goals**.
- **EXECUTE** changes necessary to remain on course to realize the **goals**.

PLANE Spending Analysis: Five questions to answer before you commit to any major expenditure:

P   Did I **Plan** this expenditure and did I include it in my budget?

L   Will the expenditure increase my **Loans**?

A   Are there realistic **Alternatives** to achieve my spending objective?

N   Is the expenditure **Necessary** to achieve my spending objective?

E   Is this the most **Effective** use of resources now, relative to my **life goals and budget goals**?

Contents

        What Is Money?
        Three Key Truths From The Bible About Money
        Think About This
        Chapter Notes

        Planned Obsolescence
        Greed
        Think About This
        Chapter Notes

        You Need An SOS!
        Three Critical Money Management Steps
        Think About This
        Chapter Notes

        Borrowing
        Getting Out Of Debt
        Interest
        Inflation

Section III: Selected Spending Decisions . 129

Section IV: Looking Beyond the Sunset . 163

Foreword

Growing up in a home with an accounting-trained father offered opportunities to learn about money from an early age. My brother and I were entrusted with allowances when we were old enough. We earned money for "jobs" at home which were above and beyond the call of duty. I remember having a bankbook and how much I enjoyed watching my money grow.

Unfortunately, after moving to Canada and discovering the wonders of the shopping mall, my money management skills fell into disuse. Now, as a young married couple in the 21st century, managing money for God's glory is increasingly difficult. Our generation has such easy access to marketing and credit, that it is often hard to determine what are needs and what are wants. This, combined with declining interest rates, has made it much less attractive to save money in the same way as our parents.

In this book, you will find that God's truth concerning money comes across loud and clear. Most importantly, you will be encouraged that no matter how big a hole you have fallen into, it is possible to get out. Despite our pre-marriage counseling sessions, my husband and I have not always made the best choices financially. However, that is in the past, and it is never too late to start making good decisions concerning our finances. I trust that you, the reader, will also experience a sense of hope and confidence in our Lord Jesus, that He is truly able to help you out of whatever situation you find yourself in.

Keisha Matheuszik
Oakville, Ontario

Acknowledgements

When I started this project, I had one key objective: to cherish every moment of interviewing, researching and writing that it involved and not focus on the end! I thank the Lord Jesus Christ for honouring this request.

Many individuals contributed to this book, but I will mention only a few. My gratitude to those not mentioned here is just as deep as to those named. Our four adult children had a significant positive influence on this book. Thank you, Bill (son-in-law) and Keisha (daughter) Matheuszik for planting the seed and for guidance along the way. Shabbir (son) and Lesley (daughter-in-law) Bell, particularly in the early stages, offered invaluable encouragement and advice. Thank you so much.

Keisha, truly I am grateful that you took time from your busy schedule with the "Twins!" to review this book and to write the foreword. I am deeply honoured.

My mother taught me accounting and budgeting skills during summer holidays in my teens. My sister, Lilibeth, Chris Barnes, and Greg Hazle assisted in different but important ways. I am grateful to you all.

Finally, my friend of forty years and my wife of thirty, Doreen, you were and continue to be magnificent! Self-described exhibit "A" for this project, you listened to my presentations so many times, read several drafts of this book, yet each time was like the first time! You were joyful, ensuring always that I kept the text simple because "the reader will be persons like me who dislike figures." You prayed continually and did so many others things. Honey, thanks so much!

To God be the glory!

Introduction

For almost thirty years, I have worked in the finance function of a large Canadian multinational group of companies. For about twenty of those years, I served as the Chief Financial Officer of different companies within the group. Early in my career, I decided to custom fit to the household budget some policies and practices from the workplace.

In 1989, my daughter, Keisha, got engaged and asked for financial counselling for her and fiancé, Bill. Unwittingly, this started the custom-fitting! Since then, I have had the privilege of working with several people, helping them to prepare and to implement spending plans, savings plans, and other financial decisions. Always, the pervasive lack of knowledge of basic money management principles and practices surprised me. I realized then that this lack of skills contributed substantially to the alarming debt rate among the young and not so young persons whom I counselled. Clearly, our Sunday Schools, churches, and high schools are not teaching basic financial skills!

During numerous trans-Pacific business trips over the past ten years, I used time in airport lounges, on planes, and in hotel rooms to develop a counselling package and material for small-group seminars on Money Management. This book synthesizes information from both counselling sessions and seminars. Additionally, it reflects:

- My training as a professional accountant;
- My education and experience as a manager;
- Key Truths from the Bible;

- Effective financial concepts and practices from my work experience designed specifically to help individuals to implement these truths; and most importantly,
- My walk with the Lord Jesus Christ.

My goal now is to present these Key Truths and concepts to help you develop an attitude towards money and spending that will honour God and that will assist you in controlling money. I do not claim that the skills and tools I propound will allow you to become rich in material terms. Truly, I do not have the ability to do this!

The Bible does not promise that material riches will flow directly from our efforts! I disagree with Christians who say that if we are good stewards of God's resources He will bless us always with wealth. He may! His will for each of us is different. The Bible shows examples of people blessed with wealth and otherwise.

I commend you to read about the lives of David and Job. In 1st and 2nd Samuel, and in the book of Job, both in the Old Testament of the Bible, we see two individuals who had hearts for God and who sought always to do His will. He blessed them with wealth. However, it was different with the twelve apostles whom Jesus chose! He did not bless them with material things! Their blessing came from experiencing the reality of the life of Jesus Christ. The richness that results from seeking first His Kingdom and His righteousness, and honouring our Lord with our finances is not necessarily material! There may be other blessings, such as having grandchildren!

We must ensure that money serves us and not vice versa. Read what Jesus said in Matthew 6:24-33:

"No one can serve two masters; for a slave will either hate the one and love the other, or be devoted to the one and despise the other. You cannot serve God and wealth. Therefore I tell you, do not worry about your life, what you will eat or what you will drink, or about your body, what you will wear. Is not life more than food, and the body more than clothing? Look at the birds of the air; they neither sow nor reap nor gather into barns, and yet your heavenly Father feeds them. Are you not of more value than they? And can any of you by worrying add a single hour to your span of life? And why do you worry about clothing? Consider the lilies of the field, how they grow; they neither toil nor spin, yet I tell you, even Solomon in all his glory was not clothed like one of these. But if God so clothes the grass of the field, which is alive today and tomorrow is thrown into the oven, will he not much more clothe you—you of little faith? Therefore do not worry, saying, 'What will we eat?' or 'What will we drink?' or 'What will we wear?' For it is the Gentiles who strive for all these things; and indeed your heavenly Father knows that you need all these things. But strive first for the kingdom of God and his righteousness, and all these things will be given to you as well."

In Matthew 19:24 **(NIV)**, referring to the wealthy unbeliever whose heart condition was to acquire more wealth for his own purposes, Jesus said "...it is easier for a camel to go through the eye of a needle than a rich man to enter the kingdom of God."

I think this book fills a void in financial fundamentals in the Christian financial management literature. It attempts to cover the issues that people face daily. I pray that after you read these pages, you will become good managers of God's resources and that you will experience His richest blessings.

Throughout this book, I have used "his" and "her" interchangeably.

Tables and Figures

Tables

Figures

Section I

Three Key Truths

To Depend on Jesus to Satisfy Our Needs
Means More Than
Crying Out to Him When We Need Help.
Accepting Him as Our Lord and Our Saviour
and Walking in Obedience
to His Will
Truly is the Answer!

1

Money and Three Key Truths

Money management is a journey that reflects our values and our lifestyles. It is not a destination! In Luke 14:28 **(RSV),**[1] speaking about the cost of becoming a disciple, Jesus said, "For which of you, desiring to build a tower, does not first sit down and count the cost, whether he has enough to complete it?"

We must evaluate the implications of our decisions before committing to any path. Accordingly, prior to starting this tour on learning to manage God's money, "count the cost"!

As the journey begins, you should know that nothing is impossible with God....[2]

- You may be in debt.
- You may think you made mistakes managing money; maybe you did! We all do!
- Focus now on learning to apply, to the future, the principles that I will discuss in this book.
- Try to learn from your experiences.
- Don't look back and be hard on yourself; move ahead!
- Most importantly, be **patient** and keep your **eyes riveted on the cross**, always remembering Jesus' words in Matthew 28:20: "...obey everything that I have commanded you. And remember I am with you always, to the end of the age."

Now fasten your seat belt and let's go!

What is Money?

Money is mentioned 112 times in the NIV Bible, 52 times in the Old Testament and 60 times in the New Testament. It is the means of exchange that replaced the barter system centuries ago. It is the instrument we use to pay for things we buy: cash, cheques, credit cards, debit cards, and loans from banks, private sources, merchants, and others.

Money will be different in the future. We will spend **electronic money** (primarily **"smart cards"**) that functions like today's credit and debit cards. Indeed, we may not see coins, paper, or bankbooks! This could happen sooner rather than later; observe the proliferation of telephone banking, Internet banking, and so on!

A London Newspaper offered a prize for the best definition of money. The prize was awarded to a young man who sent in this definition: 'Money is an article which may be used as the universal passport to every-where except heaven, and as a universal provider for everything except happiness.[3]

Three Key Truths From the Bible About Money

To manage God's money effectively, we must apply **Three Key Truths** from the Bible which, collectively, I call the **GAS** principle:

Key Truth #1: **G**od Owns Everything
Key Truth #2: **A**ccept What You Have
Key Truth #3: **S**eek First His Kingdom and Sub-
                    mit Your Requests to Him

Key Truth #1: God Owns Everything

- The earth is the LORD's and all that is in it, the world, and those who live in it; for he has founded it on the seas, and established it on the rivers.[4]

- For in him all things in heaven and on earth were created, things visible and invisible, whether thrones or dominions or rulers or powers—all things have been created through him and for him.[5]

Key Truth #2: Accept What You Have

- For we brought nothing into the world, so that we can take nothing out of it; but if we have food and clothing, we will be content with these.[6]

- Keep your lives free from the love of money, and be content with what you have; for he has said, "I will never leave you or forsake you." [7]

Key Truth #3: Seek First His Kingdom and Submit Your Requests to Him

- But seek first his kingdom and his righteousness, and all these things shall be yours as well.[8]
- Many are the plans in a man's heart, but it is the LORD's purpose that prevails.[9]

These are not subjective, changing principles. They are eternal! We must seek constantly to understand them and to find what pleases God by studying the Bible. There we will uncover lasting guidelines for daily living.

God is the creator of the universe and the owner of all we hold. The Bible demonstrates this clearly in the verses that expound the **GAS** principle, and elsewhere.

Accepting this principle will change our view of the things we "own" and the loans we incur as follows:

- We will acknowledge that we "own" nothing and that we are mere managers or stewards of God's resources;
- We will become more careful with our spending decisions; and
- We will understand that ultimately we must account to the owner of all resources, Jesus Christ, for each of our expenditures!

While jogging one morning, this word picture came to me; it has reinforced my view of the practical application of Key Truth #3 of the GAS principle: Do your best and leave the rest to God.

You are on a plane going from Montreal to Toronto, normally a one-hour flight. Your son, Bill, the First Officer, invites you to sit on the flight deck in the Jump Seat directly behind the Captain. You are flustered and know that you will be late for your first meeting in Toronto because a major snowstorm in Montreal delayed the flight.

As the plane gets airborne, you close your eyes and try to relax. After what seemed like two hours, and indeed was two hours, you open your eyes and realize that the plane has not landed. You say to Bill: "Why have we not landed in Toronto after two hours of flying?'"The Captain replies: "Don't worry, relax; we will take you to your destination!" Totally stressed out, you whisper to yourself: "Oh, God, help me please, I am so late for my meetings!" Again you close your eyes, and you notice that your heart is racing!

After about five minutes, you open your eyes and ask: "Captain, what is the problem?" The Captain turns and looks at you. There is a glow around Him! He smiles and replies, "Son, you called! Here I am! Rest in peace! The Word says:

- Call and I will answer (Jeremiah 33:3).
- Ask and you will receive (Matthew 7:7).
- Trust in Me and I will make your path straight (Proverbs 3:5-6).
- Enter My presence daily (1 Thessalonians 5:17-18).
- Rest I will give you, just come (Matthew 11:28)."

Overcome with joy, you close your eyes, smile and mutter: "Jesus, take control. I surrender all to You! Wherever You go, I will go."

Think About This

"A man who was merely a man and said the sort of things Jesus said would not be a great moral teacher. He would either be a lunatic—on a level with the man who says he is a poached egg—or else he would be the Devil of Hell. You must make your choice. Either this man was, and is, the Son of God: or else a madman or something worse."[10]

Chapter Notes:

[1] **RSV** refers to the Holy Bible: The Revised Standard Version. (Copyright © 1946, 1952, 1959, 1973 by the Division of Christian Education of the National Council of the Churches of Christ in the United States of America. All rights reserved.)

[2] Jeremiah 32:17,27; Luke 18:27

[3] Glen V. Wheeler, 1010 Illustrations, Poems and Quotes (Cincinnati, Ohio: Standard Publishing, 1967) p. 265.

[4] Psalm 24:1-2

[5] Colossians 1:16

[6] 1 Timothy 6:7-8

[7] Hebrews 13:5

[8] Matthew 6:33, **RSV**

[9] Proverbs 19:21, **NIV**

[10] C.S. Lewis, Mere Christianity (New York: The MacMillan Company, 1960) pp.40-41.

2

Why Don't We Manage Money Effectively?

What's the problem? Why don't we manage money effectively based on the **GAS** principle? I suggest two reasons:

- Planned Obsolescence
- Greed

Planned Obsolescence

Welcome to the world of planned obsolescence where companies' products have short life cycles. Regularly, businesses introduce to the market new goods and services and upgrades to existing goods and services. Each introduction improves existing versions, thereby producing better and faster (where relevant) products.

To support this rapid pace of obsolescence, corporations use aggressive and sophisticated marketing to convince us to buy their goods and services. They supply credit, usually expensive, and they make shopping convenient via the Internet, the telephone, and the television. They capture our imagination, and their sales soar!

We experience this phenomenon by the frequency with which we renew or replace our computers and accessories, cars, clothes, "grown-up toys" (video games, mobile phones, beepers, organizers, sports cars), and other stuff! Why do we respond to these dazzling advertising campaigns with credit we can't afford? We had no problem with our computers, our cars, and our "grown-up toys" before their suppliers convinced us that we needed to change them!

I suggest that we respond this way because the **GAS** principle is not instinctive. I urge you to exercise faith now and begin studying and practising this principle so that it becomes automatic. Then you will evaluate and discard quickly alluring marketing campaigns designed to seduce you to spend God's money unwisely!

Greed

I have described the external influences. What about the internal forces? Greed, I suggest, is the reason **commercials** and **infomercials** attract us. This is what Jesus said about greed in Luke 12:15:

> And he said to them, "Take care! Be on your guard against all kinds of greed; for one's life does not consist in the abundance of possessions."

Paul's message in Colossians 3:5 also is profound: Put to death, therefore, whatever in you is earthly: fornication, impurity, passion, evil desire, and greed (which is idolatry).

The Concise Oxford Dictionary of Current English, 9th Edition, defines greed as: "Intense or excessive desire especially for food or wealth." We display this excessive desire for wealth when we do the following:

- Give telephone-marketers **our bank account or credit card numbers** in exchange for prizes that never materialize!
- Attend seminars teaching us how to **get rich effortlessly**!
- Buy **lottery tickets**!

William Wilberforce, the Philanthropist and Reformer who led the fight to abolish slavery in Britain, once said: "I continually find it necessary to guard against that natural love of wealth and grandeur which prompts us always, when we come to apply our general doctrine to our own case, to claim an exception." [1]

I spend many hours at various international airports, and I am amazed at the number of books I see which propose formulas for getting rich quickly and easily! Similarly, I have seen advertisements for several seminars where presenters claimed to have the "get rich quickly and effortlessly" recipe! Regrettably, people reply to these invitations; some lose their small savings in the process!

In his book, Just Rewards,[2] David Olive wrote:

At a conference on Native Canadian business enterprises in 1986, Barbara McDougall, then minister of state for finance, celebrated the rise of Native-owned businesses. 'There's one underlying motive in business shared by all—it's greed,' said McDougall, who once worked in the securities industry....

Olive mentioned also that Toronto financier Conrad Black told Peter Newman that, *"Greed has been severely under-estimated and denigrated. There is nothing wrong with avarice as a motive, as long as it doesn't lead to anti-social conduct."* Olive commented on these and other statements that "greed does bring out the worst in people—and in corporations." To be sure, it does!

How widespread is this desire to get rich quickly? The September 13, 1999 edition of Business Week carried an article titled, "US$ 276 million: Now That's Motivation," which states:

> ...No doubt there is potential to be mined in self-improvement and personal enrichment—the market accounts for more than US$ 7 billion in video, book, and other sales....

Each of us must develop a strong, personal relationship with Jesus Christ and stay in His Word to repel the greed trait. Otherwise, we will continue to react to suppliers' appeal to this characteristic, and ultimately, we will abuse credit by doing the following:

- Maintaining credit card balances and paying exorbitant interest charges;
- Buying now with the intent to pay later, but not providing for the later payment;
- Taking advances against insurance policies;
- Borrowing from all conceivable sources;

- Consolidating all loans and continuing our spending spree, instead of changing our *attitude* and *behaviour* towards money.

Eventually, the volcano of debt that lay dormant for years will erupt and remain active!

Think About This

Have you ever computed the amount of money you would save if you eliminated from your monthly expenses the things that are "nice to have" but are not "necessary"?

Chapter Notes:

[1] William Wilberforce, "Money in Christian History," Christian History, no. 14.

[2] David Olive, Just Rewards (Toronto: Key Porter Books Limited, 1987) pp. 23-24.

3

How to Control Money

To manage God's money effectively, you need an **SOS!**

Stop striving for more and accept what you have! With the help of our Lord Jesus Christ, **you** decide, not merchants:

- What **you** need.
- When **you** need it.
- How **you** will pay for it.

Proverbs 3:5-6 tells us to "Trust in the LORD with all your heart, and do not rely on your own insight. In all your ways acknowledge him, and he will make straight your paths." Do your best and let God do the rest!

Own **your** present financial situation and apply **self-control.**

> Galatians 5:22-23 says: *"By contrast, the fruit of the Spirit is love, joy, peace, patience, kindness, generosity, faithfulness, gentleness, and self-control. There is no law against such things."*

- **Understand** where **you** are.
- **Don't rationalize** and make excuses for your situation.
- **Don't blame** anyone.
- **Decide** to change.
- **Don't borrow** to increase your spending power as a way out.

> Remember Jesus' words in Matthew 11:28 **(NIV)**: *"Come to me, all you who are weary and burdened, I will give you rest."*

Start now to get to know and follow the **Shepherd** and to apply the **GAS** principle. Shortly, we shall explore how:

The
Shepherd
gives
Gas
for
Peace[1]
on the
Plane[2]

You need to take **three critical steps** to start this biblically-based money management trip, a schematic of which I show in Appendix 1:

- Establish where you are with the Shepherd—your **"Eternal Worth."**
- Establish where you are with God's resources—your **"Material Worth."**
- Set long and short-term life goals—your **"Destination."**

Critical Money Management Step #1: Get to Know the Shepherd

- Jesus Christ is the Good Shepherd.
- We are His sheep.
- He died and rose again and is alive today.

In John 10:27-30, Jesus said:

"My sheep hear my voice. I know them, and they follow me. I give them eternal life, and they will never perish. No one will snatch them out of my hand. What my Father has given me is greater than all else, and no one can snatch it out of the Father's hand. The Father and I are one."

Before proceeding, answer this question: **Is Jesus Christ your Lord and your Saviour?** To initiate the **Gas** principle, you must know Him and His Word!

In my role as Chief Financial Officer of various subsidiaries of the company for which I work, I must know and implement the company's principles, policies, and practices. I cannot be successful otherwise. Similarly, to manage God's money effectively, you must know Him and His Word. Become Jesus' Chief Financial Officer now! Then you will spend His money based on the principles in the Bible, assured always that...

- He will never leave you nor forsake you (Hebrews 13:5).
- Nothing is impossible for Him (Matthew 19:26).
- One day you will account to Him (Matthew 25:14-30).

A good reality check is to ask yourself these questions: **What does Jesus say when He sees...**

- My credit card statement?
- My cheque book stubs/bank statement?
- My loan payments?
- My financial affairs?

If you are uncomfortable with your answers, ask a further question: **Do I need to change my attitude and behaviour towards money?**

By now you should have established your **Eternal Worth**—your position in Jesus Christ! If you have not surrendered your life to Him already, I encourage you to turn to Chapter 16 of this book immediately, and to prayerfully "**count the cost**" of accepting Jesus Christ as your Lord and your Saviour.

I can assure you that the techniques I present in this book will help you to develop a systematic approach to managing money. Equally, I can assure you that unless you accept the **GAS** principle, which is based on accepting Christ as your Lord and Saviour, you will remain a slave to money and you will never have "enough."

Critical Money Management Step #2: Establish Where You Are With His Resources

Next, establish your net worth, or **Material Worth**, as in Table I. The **net worth statement** is a "still photograph" of your financial affairs at a specific date. It reflects what you "owned" (God owns everything, so your ownership is in the form of a Trusteeship[3]) and what you owed at that date, and is the base from which you will travel during our money management journey. If you visit a financial adviser to help you with financial matters, he will need this statement.

We show amounts under "Own" at market value,[4] not at your cost to buy them; these are your **assets**. Notice the asset called **"Personal Effects,"** which includes clothing, jewellery, paintings, and other personal items. Often we forget that we could sell some of these items. If you need cash urgently for a special expense that passes the various spending tests I will discuss later, sell a component of **personal effects**.

Indeed, to reduce your debts, consider selling any other item from the "Own" side that you do not require. However, do not make this decision lightly.

The total of each side of the statement is $199,000, but the "Equity" on the "Owe" side is a mere $38,500 because you used loans (other individuals' money) to buy most of the assets! Items on your "Owe" side are your **liabilities**.

Table I: Net Worth Statement
(as at 30 June 1999)

"Own" (Assets)		"Owe" (Liabilities)	
Car	$9,000	Car Loan	$11,000
House	$150,000	Mortgage	$125,000
Furniture	$20,000	Credit Card	$20,000
Personal Effects	**$15,000**	Family loan	$2,000
Other	$5,000	Other loans	$2,500
Sub-Total	$199,000	**Total Loans**	**$160,500**
		Equity	**$38,500**
Total	$199,000	Total	$199,000

Critical Money Management Step #3: Establish Life Goals

It's game seven of the Stanley Cup finals at the Molson Centre in Montreal. The Vancouver Canucks meet the Montreal Canadiens with the series tied at 3-3. It's game time and the players face-off. Montreal gets the puck and, in a series of brilliantly executed plays (yes, I am biased!), a Montreal player prepares to shoot the puck. Abruptly, he and all other players start yelling at the referee: There are no nets on the ice! How do we score a goal? No nets, no goaltenders, what's the purpose of this game?

When you go through life without setting goals, how do you score a goal? The third step to managing God's money is to establish **Life Goals**. Your vital, eternal goal should be to develop **a vibrant relationship with Jesus Christ**. The corresponding "material" goal should be **debt-free living**. **Life Goals** are essential because they...

- Help you to set priorities, both short-term and long-term; if you do not know where you wish to go, **you will get there!**

- Help to separate "needs" from "wants"; if you do not know how to separate needs from wants, money will control you as manufacturers seduce you with excellent advertising campaigns!

- Allow you to select the best alternative to fulfill your needs; if you do not set goals, you will lose options the closer you get to the event!

Before you finalize your goals, submit them to the Lord. Ask Him to direct you to the Word as you seek His will. Here are examples of "material" life goals:

Long-Term Goals

- Early retirement
- Children's education or personal education
- Early repayment of total mortgage/debt-free lifestyle
- Investments/Savings

Short-Term Goals

- Vacation
- Repayment of credit card debt
- Savings

Financial Health Goals

- Maximum Debt Ratio[5]
- Debt Repayment Ratio[6]

Naturally, each person will develop goals that are relevant to her. I suggest that you seek God's will for you in this process.

Individuals do not normally set **Financial Health Goals**, though they tend to hear about rough guidelines for housing expenses. Currently, you would not expect your mortgage repayment (principal and interest) plus taxes and utilities, as a percent of your gross income, to exceed 30%. When you go shopping for a house, the real estate agent would probably mention this.

I recommend a more comprehensive approach to financial health goals. Each person (for singles) or each family (for married couples) should establish these goals as part of a total money management system. Couples should pool their incomes and compute one number for each of the two ratios. Successful companies establish and adhere to various financial goals routinely. I suggest that the absence (among other things) of the discipline of establishing and following broad financial health goals is a major reason for many individuals and families to drift into the ocean of major debt.

In the net worth statement above, total loans were $160,500, representing 81% of total assets of

$199,000. Clearly this is too high a **Maximum Debt Ratio**! Set the **Maximum Debt Ratio** goal in conjunction with the **Debt Repayment Ratio**. Each person/family must decide on the borrowing level that will eliminate stress and will conform to the **GAS** and other principles we discuss in this book.

Think About This

Did you know that your expenses tend to rise as your income increases? The more you earn, the more you will spend! To have funds available to use for the Lord's work, you must spend consistently less than you earn.

Chapter Notes:

[1] *PEACE Budgetary Control System* (Copyright © 1994-1999, Michel A. Bell).

[2] *PLANE Spending Analysis* (Copyright © 1997, Michel A. Bell).

[3] A Trustee is a person who has legal title to property that he uses for another persons' benefit.

[4] Market value is the amount someone may pay for an item; not what you think it should be worth.

[5] **Maximum Debt Ratio** represents the **total of all loans** on the net worth statement **($160,500)** as a percentage of the total liabilities ("Owe") side of the net worth statement **($199,000). For this person it was (160,500/199,000) × 100 = 81% at 30 June 1999.**

[6] The **Debt Repayment Ratio** is the total loan payments (including mortgage principal and interest) for the period (one year) as a percentage of gross income for the period.

4

Elements of Finance 101

In this chapter, I discuss the following financial concepts that support the **PEACE** Budgetary Control System **("PEACE")** which I explain in Section II:

- **Borrowing**
- **Getting Out of Debt**
- **Interest**
- **Inflation**
- **The Value of Money**
- **Cash Flows**
- **Tax Shield**

Borrowing

Household borrowing in Canada **increased** to $13.1 billion in the **first half of 1997** ($1.3 billion higher than in the corresponding period in 1996), as low interest rates and improving consumer confidence stimulated consumer borrowing to finance the purchase of durables. Household debt as a percentage of personal **disposable income**[1] **climbed to 97%** by mid-1997, moving from 93% in 1995.[2]

Bankruptcies[3] are rising in Canada, among other things, because of the proliferation of credit card usage, rising cost of education, and downsizing of large corporations. Between 1966 and 1996, consumer bankruptcies grew 13.3% per year while business bankruptcies rose by 5.6%. In 1996, 80,000 consumers went bankrupt owing a total of $1.9 billion![4]

You must control money to escape this debt trap! Strive to be debt-free, remembering always that it is God's money. When you borrow, you assume that you will earn a certain income in the future to repay the loan. This is not a good assumption, as you do not know the future! **James 4:13-17** cautions as follows:

> *Come now, you who say, "Today or tomorrow we will go to such and such a town and spend a year there, doing business and making money." Yet you do not even know what tomorrow will bring. What is your life? For you are a mist that appears for a little while and then vanishes. Instead you ought to say, "If the Lord wishes, we will live and do this or that." As it is, you boast in your arrogance; all such boasting is evil. Anyone, then, who knows the right thing to do and fails to do it, commits sin.*

Proverbs 22:7, *"The rich rules over the poor, and the borrower is the slave of the lender,"* is food for thought. I am sure you have seen several examples that confirm this statement! Generally, borrow to buy a home only; and then only after establishing your **financial health goals**. Save to buy all other items! After I say this, participants in my seminars normally ask, "What happens if I 'need' a car and I have not saved for it?" As you ponder this question, I assure you that I will discuss it in Section II when I explain the **Affordability Index**.

Two forms of borrowing, both of which tend to be more expensive than available alternatives, have become acceptable to many individuals: leasing a car and maintaining credit card balances.

Leasing a car can be an expensive alternative to borrowing to purchase the car. Before leasing, unless you are comfortable with financial analyses, consult a fee only or independent financial adviser to perform a "lease versus buy" analysis, which I describe in Section III.

Maintaining credit card balance(s) is the other popular but expensive form of borrowing! In August 1999, the interest rate on some credit card balances was about 18.5% per year. Then, a Line of Credit[5] from a major bank attracted 7.75% while the interest rate on car loans from banks varied between 8.5 to 10%, and from some car dealerships between 8 to 9%. Therefore, pay your credit card balances in full always, and save toward all purchases. Remember you do not need...

- The best of everything;
- To upgrade your home or your car;

...and

- Your lifestyle has a specific cost;
- Your lifestyle impacts others around you and is a witness of your walk with God.

How does this advice on borrowing compare with what Paul said in 1 Timothy 5:8? Paul said, *"And whoever does not provide for relatives, and especially for family members, has denied the faith and is worse than an unbeliever."*

He states clearly that you have a responsibility, heads of households, to provide for your families. However, you must discharge this duty consistent with God's Word by adhering to the **GAS** principle and other biblical advice on borrowing.

There may be instances when you think you must borrow to provide for your family. When these arise, I urge you strongly never to borrow as a first option. Follow the **GAS** principle and seek earnestly to know God's will for you. He may be taking you and your family through the "refiner's fire" to "purify" you.[6] You wouldn't want to miss the ensuing benefits!

Ultimately, before you decide to borrow, start to follow the **PEACE** Budgetary Control system, the **PLANE** Spending Analysis, and the **Affordability Index** that I outline in Section II. Ask, "What would Jesus do?"

An important principle that should underpin every decision to borrow is this: **If you borrow, you must ensure repayment.** Psalm 37:21 states that, *"The wicked borrow, and do not pay back, but the righteous are generous and keep giving."* When you act as a guarantor[7] for someone's loan, effectively you become a lender! Read what Proverbs 11:15 says: *"To guarantee loans for a stranger brings trouble, but there is safety in refusing to do so."* Reflect on this when someone asks you to co-sign a loan.

I would like to dispel this myth about borrowing: Borrow as early in life as possible merely to establish your credit history. Nonsense! Don't borrow to establish a credit history. Your best credit history is one that reads: **Never Borrowed!** During counselling sessions, many persons said the reason they borrowed initially was to establish credit ratings. They did not **need** to borrow then! Usually, this first borrowing started the addiction to using credit cards and not paying their full monthly balances.

Consider also that interest paid to service loans reduces available funds from your household budget, thereby reducing funds available to do "kingdom" building!

Getting Out of Debt

What happens when you start this money management journey deeply in debt? Sadly, many persons whom I counsel do. Already they have stopped tithing and have one major request: "Please help me to consolidate all my debts into one." Normally, I offer this advice:

First, ensure you are walking with the Lord.

- **Seek after the Lord. Cling to His words** and He will make your path straight (Proverbs 3:5-6).
- **Examine your prayer life**: Have you been communing regularly with God?
- **Examine your "spiritual diet"**: Have you been spending time in His Word?
- **Examine your church life**: Have you been attending church and fellowshipping with believers?
- **Restore your tithing** and other giving immediately.
- Determine to **change your attitude and behaviour** towards money now.

- Try to understand what got you into this situation. Predictably, this person has not been budgeting and has been spending freely on his credit card.

- Examine your expenses over the past six months to see where the money went.

- Prepare your net worth statement to determine if you have assets that you can sell to reduce your debts.

- Establish **Life Goals**.

- "Cut up" all credit cards now.

- See an independent financial adviser to assist you to prepare a "zero-based" budget (a budget in which every expenditure is based on an actual NEED) and a revival plan showing detailed steps to get out of debt. This may include letters to creditors requesting lower interest rates and other concessions.

- Start to implement the **PEACE** system that is the subject of Section II of this book.

- Become accountable to someone you can trust for following the "revival plan."

- Although listed last, this is important: You got into debt over time, you will get out in time by the grace of God. **Be Patient! Remember, nothing is impossible for God!**

Interest

Interest is the cost you pay to a lender for money he advanced to you. The flip side is interest received on deposits with banks or financial institutions. The concept of interest has been around for a long time. All of the ten Old Testament references (in the **NIV**) counsel lenders against either charging interest on loans to the poor or charging excessive interest.

The only New Testament reference is in the Parable of the Talents in Matthew 25:27 and Luke 19:23. The essence of this parable is neither about money nor banking. Warren Wiersbe, in his "Be" series[8] on the New Testament, states that the talents represent opportunities to use our abilities; we have been assigned ministries according to these abilities and gifts that God has given to us. "It is our privilege to serve the Lord and multiply His goods," he says.

The servant in the parable did nothing with his talent; probably thinking it was so small it would make no difference. In the eyes of our Lord, nothing is too small. Consequently, the master in the parable told the servant who hid his one talent in the ground: *"Then you ought to have invested my money with the bankers, and on my return I would have received what was my own with interest."*

Let's get back to interest. We deposit funds with institutions, confident that they are secure. We do not care (many of us do not know) that banks do not keep all our money in their vaults. They lend more money than they take in! When the bank or financial institution receives a deposit, by law it must keep a small percentage, but it will lend the majority to you, someone else, or me ("borrower"). To the depositor, the bank will pay a rate of interest (say 5%) which is lower than the rate of interest it receives (say 9%) from the borrower. The difference of 4% is the "spread" that the bank keeps as a part of its profit.

Apart from the spread, the interest rate that the financial institutions charge on loans reflects some of these elements:

- Their cost and profit;
- Their estimate of the risk of non-payment (the higher the risk, the higher the interest rate charged);
- Their view of the quality of security provided by borrower (the closer to cash, the better for them);
- Your credit history;
- The purpose of the loan.

Inflation

Does inflation affect the rate of interest we receive from banks and other financial institutions on our savings? To be sure it does! Inflation is a general and sustained rise in price levels in an economy. The most widely accepted measure of inflation is the Consumer Price Index (CPI).

A CPI is a means to measure the total change in the prices of retail goods and services that we buy. The measurement is done over a specific period (one month) and for a precise basket of goods and services. If the CPI was set at 100 in 1990 and rose to 150 in 1998, prices of goods and services in the basket would have increased by 50% over that period. Normally, governments maintain the CPI for different regions and nationally.

Although inflation is currently under control in Canada and in the USA, still you must know its impact, because it can raise its ugly head any time. If your savings earn less than the rate of inflation, you lose spending power. If you receive 5% on your bank deposits, and the inflation rate is 7%, you would be worse off because prices were rising faster (7%) than your savings (5%). This is significant as you prepare your financial plan and start to think about retirement income. The difference between the actual interest rate and the rate of inflation is the "real interest" rate. This is the relevant interest rate for you. In our example it is negative (5% - 7% = -2%).

The Value of Money

Because of inflation, and interest on money that you will either receive or pay, $100 today normally is not worth the same as $100 you will receive in the future. If you deposited today's $100 at 5% interest, at the end of one year it would be worth $105 ($100 + $5 interest). If you left it for another year, it would become $110.25 ($105 + $5.25 interest). Notice that in the second year, in addition to interest on the original deposit of $100, you received interest also on the first year's interest of $5. This is **compound interest**— receiving or paying interest on interest.

One dollar (or any amount) will double at the end of 14, 10, and 8 years if the annual rates of interest are 5%, 7%, and 9% respectively. Table II shows how one dollar will grow (compound) when the interest earned is reinvested; a $10 deposit would produce ten times those numbers, $20 twenty times, and so on.

Table II: Growth of $1 With Interest Reinvested

Years From Now	Annual Rate of Return		
	5%	10%	15%
1	1.05	1.10	1.15
2	1.10	1.21	1.32
3	1.16	1.33	1.52
4	1.22	1.46	1.75
5	1.28	1.61	2.01
10	1.63	2.59	4.05
14	2.00	3.80	7.08
15	2.08	4.18	8.14
20	2.65	6.73	16.37
25	3.39	10.83	32.92

If you had to decide between $100 now and $110 in two years at 5% interest rate, you would be indifferent. Both have the same value today. Thus, the **present value** or today's value of $110 (**the future value**) to be received in two years is $100. This present value idea is important when you have to choose between spending or receiving money now or later; such as buying extended warranties, repaying loans early, or comparing buying versus leasing decisions. For these choices, compare always the present values of each option.

Suppose you had an option to repay a loan of $2000. If repaid now you would be allowed a discount of 15%, but if paid at the end of one year, you would have to pay the full amount plus 5%. How do you evaluate these options? You must compare the present values (today's values) of each as follows:

- The present value of a payment of $2000 now less 15% discount is $2000 - (2000 × 15%) = $1700
- The present value of a payment of $2000 to be made one year hence at 5% interest is $2000. The value at the end of one year would be $2100, which is $2000 plus 5% of $2000, or $100.

If you had the funds you would repay this loan now because you would save $300 ($2000 - $1700).

In Table III, you see another and more powerful example of compound interest. Here you save one dollar each year plus accumulated interest. At the end of ten years, the value would have grown to $13.18 at an interest rate of 6% per year. If you had saved $100 instead of $1, the value at year ten would be $1300.18 and so on. In Section II, when I discuss the need to save, do remember Tables II and III.

Table III: Growth From Saving $1 Every Year

Years From Now	Annual Rate of Return		
	6%	10%	15%
1	1.00	1.00	1.00
2	2.06	2.10	2.15
3	3.18	3.31	3.47
4	4.37	4.64	4.99
5	5.64	6.10	6.74
10	13.18	15.94	20.30
15	23.27	31.77	47.58
20	36.78	57.27	102.44
25	43.39	98.34	212.77

Cash Flows

Earlier, we saw a net worth statement, which I described as a "still photograph" of what you owned (assets) and what you owed (liabilities). Obviously, it changes when you receive income, pay expenses, repay debts, or buy or sell assets. To capture these changes, we need a "video camera" that we call a "cash flow" statement.

We divide this statement into two segments—Inflows and Outflows, as in Table IV. Inflows, as the name implies, show **cash received**, and **outflows reflect cash paid.** You must know the timing of receipts and payment to prepare a cash flow statement for future expenses as in Table IV.

You have all the facts to prepare this statement! No consultant will have this information. Initially, the idea of you preparing a cash flow statement will seem daunting to you! However, the mystique goes when you realize that it shows merely the timing of funds you plan to get and to spend, and the net balance.

What conclusions can we draw from this cash flow statement? Do the October and November balances indicate that you will have surplus cash to spend or save? Not necessarily! You must review total estimated spending over a longer period and reserve money to pay those expenses which occur irregularly, such as car maintenance, Christmas gifts, and so on. You must ensure that you do not spend cash that builds up during the year unless you have used the **PEACE** system and it showed that you had a genuine cash surplus.

The cash flow statement is another key report that we will use to prepare your budget. Ideally, we would wish to construct a cash flow statement for the twelve months of the upcoming budget period to see the timing of our projected spending.

Table IV

Cash Flow Statement, Oct–Dec '98				
INFLOWS	Oct	Nov	Dec	Total
Gross Salaries	3150	3150	3150	9450
Interest income	11	11	11	33
Less: Tithe 10% of gross salaries	(315)	(315)	(315)	(945)
Less: Income taxes & other deductions	(885)	(885)	(885)	(2655)
Total Inflows	**1961**	**1961**	**1961**	**5883**
OUTFLOWS				
Capital Fund	150	150	150	450
Rent	500	500	500	1500
Car Expenses— Loan repayment	300	300	300	900
Car Expenses— Gasoline	75	45	90	210
Car Expenses— Maintenance	0	0	90	90
Telephone	30	40	65	135
Recreation	125	160	200	485
Groceries	350	300	450	1100
Gifts	0	0	40	40
Total Outflows	**1530**	**1495**	**1885**	**4910**
Net Cash flow	**431**	**466**	**76**	**973**

Tax Shield

The tax shield is the tax you recover from certain expenditures. Generally, if you earned $1667 per month and your top or marginal income tax rate was 40%, your after tax income would be $1000. Therefore, to spend $100 for an item for which you do not get a tax benefit, you must earn $167 and pay taxes of $67. Thus, to pay a car repair bill of $100, you must earn $167, give the government $67, then pay the garage $100.

For certain expenditures, you get a tax benefit. Here in Quebec, if I made a donation of $100 to an approved charitable organization in December, initially I must earn $167 and pay taxes, say of $67, via payroll deduction. In the following March or April, when I file my tax return, I would get a refund of $40.[9] This $40 is my tax shield; it has been sheltered from taxes! Table IV-1 shows the impact of donating $100 to an approved charitable organization and of spending $100 for car repairs.

Table IV-1

	$100 For Car Repairs	$100 Charitable Donations	$100 Donations Restated
Income earned	$167	$167	$167
Tax @ 40%	$67	$67→(67-40)	$27
Net Inc. after tax	$100	$100	$140
Payment for...			
Car Repairs	$100		
Donation		$100	$100
Cash avail. before filing tax return	0	0	
Tax refund	0	$40	$40

Tax rates will vary by Province. Remember this concept when we discuss "giving." Because of the tax shield, you may be able to give to the Lord's work more than you think!

Think About This

How much money do you think is "enough" for you? Unless you surrender your plans to Jesus Christ, you will never have "enough"! There will always be one more "need" to be satisfied!

Chapter Notes:

[1] Personal **Disposable Income** is the income you have available after taxes and payroll deductions have been taken from your salary.

[2] *Bank of Canada Review,* Autumn 1997, pp. 67.

[3] **Bankruptcy** occurs when a borrower can no longer repay amounts owing and his lenders are unwilling to modify his loans or provide more credit.

[4] Bank of Montreal Economic Analysis, *A Primer on Canadian Bankruptcies,* February 1998.

[5] **A Line of Credit** is a short-term revolving loan that banks extend to certain customers based on a minimum net worth and favourable credit rating.

[6] James 1:1-6

[7] When you guarantee a loan for someone, you undertake to repay amounts owing if that person fails to repay the loan.

[8] Warren Wiersbe's "Be" Series: NT Volumes 1 & 2 (Copyright © 1989 by SP Productions, Inc.).

[9] The Federal tax credit for charitable donations is 17% of the first $200 and 29% above $200 up to 75% of your

taxable income. For Quebec (the only Province with a separate tax department), the tax credit is 23% of taxable income to a maximum of 75% of taxable income. A donation of $100 would attract $17 (17% of $100) from the Federal Government and $23 (23% of $100) from the Quebec Government.

Section II

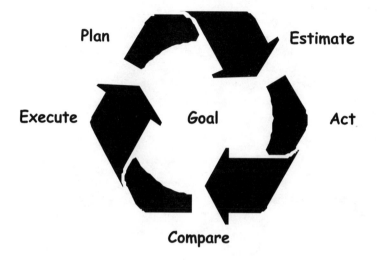

Plan

Estimate

Execute

Goal

Act

Compare

The PEACE Budgetary Control System

*Nobody But You
Can Control
Your Spending Habits*

The PEACE budget

5

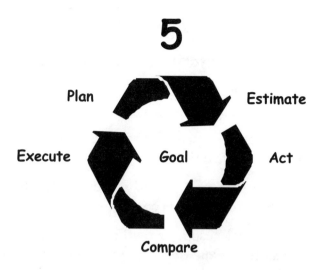

Plan   Estimate

Execute   Goal   Act

Compare

Overview of the PEACE Budgetary Control System

The next step in the money management process is to learn to use the **PEACE Budgetary Control System ("PEACE")** and supporting tools that complement the **Gas** principle. The two key analytical tools that we will review in detail are the **PLANE Spending Analysis** and the **Affordability Index**.

Here are definitions of some key words that I will be using immediately to expand the **PEACE** system:

- A **Goal** is your **destination**—where you wish to go.
- A **Plan** is your **journey**—the steps to achieve your **goal**.
- An **Estimate** is the likely cost of the **plan**—the cost of the steps in the **plans**.

- A **Budget** is a record of the results of the **planning and estimating** processes.

The PEACE Budgetary Control System

P<small>LAN</small> for a specific period to accomplish precise **goals**.

E<small>STIMATE</small> and record the expenses needed to achieve those **goals**.

A<small>CT</small> on the **plan and record** actual results as you progress toward your **goals**.

C<small>OMPARE</small> **actual** results **with** the **plan** and with the **estimated expenses** required to attain the **goals**.

E<small>XECUTE</small> changes necessary to remain on course to realize the **goals**.

The focal point of **PEACE** is accomplishment of **goals**. Each step points you to your **goal** or **goals**. It starts with developing a **plan** to achieve your pre-set **goal** or **goals** toward which you focus all related activities. Accordingly, you must evaluate all your actions throughout the **PEACE** process in the context of your **goal (or destination)!** I will develop this later, but I would like you to keep it in mind throughout this book.

Already you would have set your **Life Goals** to indicate your ultimate focus (your long-term destination). Now I will illustrate the key activities of **PEACE** that will help you to reach this destination on time and within budget.

PLAN

Deciding and recording **how** to get to your **destination**—how to achieve your **goal**. This would show intermediary stages of your journey to allow you to monitor your actual journey; e.g.

- How do I get to Vancouver from Montreal? By train, car, or by PLANE? **Assume by car.**
- What are the intermediary stops, if any? Regina? Calgary? **Assume Regina** among others.
- Where do I stay en route? **Assume several hotels** in major cities (precise details would be required).
- How long do I stay/how much spending money do I need? **Assume** the total trip is **one month** and you will spend $40 per day for food.

ESTIMATE

Costing the steps and assigning values to each intermediary stage of the journey.

- Cost of airfare, gas, train fare/accommodation. **Assume gasoline of $5 per day, hotel cost of $40 per night.**

ACT

Starting the journey with the **plan** and **estimate** as your **road map.**

- **Record your spending** on food, gasoline, hotel stay and other items, using the **same format** as for **the plan and estimate.**

COMPARE

Comparing continually, actual results with the plan and the estimate, noting carefully.

- Where you are, **compared** with where you should be according to **the road map.**
- **Actual costs**—for food, gasoline, and so on—incurred (both spent and committed[1]) to date, **compared** to the **estimated cost** up to the present stage.
- **The original estimated cost** to complete the journey per the road map, compared with your **current estimated cost** based on current knowledge.

EXECUTE

Implementing changes to allow you to complete the journey on time and within the estimated cost.

No doubt you realize that the **PEACE** system includes **two major inter-connected phases**. The **first is the Budgeting phase** that consists of the first and second steps of **PEACE—Plan** and **Estimate**. I repeat: **Life Goals** that you established earlier are essential to focus this phase of the **PEACE** system.

The second major phase includes the final three steps of **PEACE—Act, Compare, and Execute**.

The difficulty some folks have with the **PEACE** system is maintaining it. It never stops! Consequently, the **critical success factor** for these inter-connected **Budgeting** and **Control** phases (from which is derived "budgetary control") to be effective is to keep the total system going. If circumstances change, you must adjust one or a combination of the following: your **plan,** your **estimates,** or your **actions.** Each segment of **PEACE** is vital to achieve your ultimate **goal.**

Figure 1: The PEACE Budgetary Control System

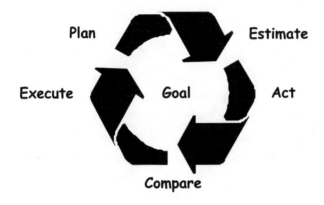

Plan

Estimate

Execute   Goal   Act

Compare

Think About This

As a baby grows older, her food must change to provide different nutrients necessary to sustain her. Similarly, the young "believer" must spend time in the Word and in prayer daily, to experience spiritual growth and the fullness of God's grace.

Chapter Notes:

[1] You must note your **commitments,** such as your decision to overnight at a hotel where you have made a non-refundable deposit. If you consider items spent only, you will forget the amounts you committed to spend and reallocate these committed amounts.

6

The Budgeting Phase of PEACE
(Planning and Estimating)

Suppose you wanted to drive from **Montreal to Vancouver**. Before starting, would you review the following details?

- How many kilometres to drive daily?
- Which famous sights to visit along the way?
- Where to overnight?
- Estimated arrival time?
- How much money to spend?

Perhaps you would **list the expenses you think** you will incur. You may add extra funds for emergencies!

En route, would you **note your spending?** Would you **compare** it **with your estimate?** To ensure you kept enough money, maybe you would! Insufficient funds might require reducing your desired frequent snacks!

Essentially, this process represents the budgetary control system I described in the previous chapter. Managing God's money effectively requires it. Surely you did not know it was that easy! Did you?

What is Budgeting?

Before examining the budgeting phase of **PEACE**, I will define budgeting. Speaking to His disciples on the cost of discipleship, Jesus illustrates vividly a key aspect of budgeting when He said:

> *"For which of you, desiring to build a tower, does not first sit down and count the cost, whether he has enough to complete it?"* (Luke 14:28, **RSV**).

Budgeting is "counting the cost"! It is systematic planning, estimating, allocating, and recording resources needed to attain your goal or set of goals.

Why Prepare a Budget?

You prepare a budget before a planned event to decide whether you will have enough funds to achieve your **goals**. Let's return to the Vancouver trip that you estimate at $500. If you had $300 only, you would start if you believed you could reduce the cost to $300. Otherwise, you would consider different options to get there, such as:

- Taking the train,
- Reducing the stay,
- Inviting a friend to share expenses, or
- Other options.

Having a pragmatic budget reduces stress and shows you the likely path ahead!

What if you did not prepare a budget? You would have selected a path without careful analysis. You may complete the trip, but you may get surprises along the way.

Suppose you started the trip without a budget and spent all the money before the end? After you start your journey, you lose expense-reducing options that were available initially. Thus, you would be forced during the journey to choose from existing options only. When you budget before you begin your journey, you have a broader range of alternative solutions from which to choose. If you did not prepare a budget and you spent all your funds mid-way, you would have a problem! You would be forced to select one of these alternatives:

- Changing your goal; you may decide not to complete the journey and borrow[1] funds to return home.
- Borrowing funds to complete the journey.

Often individuals say they prepare budgets and get no benefits. I am not surprised! A budget merely is the start of a dynamic budgetary control system. You get benefits by implementing both the **budgeting and the control** phases of the **PEACE** system.

Since God owns everything and we must seek His will, why should we plan or budget? Planning and budgeting do not take "control" from God. He gave us free wills. We must acknowledge His sovereignty and commit to Him. We should excel always within this framework while forever depending on His guidance.

Second Chronicles 20 illustrates dependence on God to play His supernatural role while we follow Him and do our best. Here we see the Moabites and others about to attack Jehoshaphat. Verse 3 **(NIV)** says *"...Alarmed, Jehoshaphat resolved to inquire of the LORD, and he proclaimed a fast...."* He agreed that this was God's battle, not his. Then he sought God's direction!

No doubt you agree that the **PEACE** system is "no big thing"! I hear this in my seminars and one-on-one counselling sessions. Folks say it is quite simple! Others complain that it requires too much discipline. That's right! It is no big thing, it is simple and it requires discipline. That's how it was designed! Essentially, I simplified proven business practices. However, there is good news! Shortly after these folks use the **PEACE** system, they start experiencing real benefits in their pocket books, and they rejoice! They identify secondary benefits of reduced stress, and for couples, fewer arguments!

If you spend money routinely, as we all do, you should budget and monitor spending. Applying the **PEACE** system not only reduces worry and stress, but it decreases surprises. You get peace (pardon the pun!) knowing you have done your best to forecast your expenses! You might dislike the results. However, you will have enough information to know the possibilities.

Specific Goals For a Budget

Besides **Life Goals**, you must decide on specific goals for the budget period. Here are two:

a) No budget deficit[2]—expenses must not exceed income; and

b) The budget should be fully funded—sufficient funds allocated to complete the journey. Otherwise, revisit the process, including examining your goals and estimates.

Accept realistic budgets only. The following may be other goals of the budgeting process:

- To take your dream "vacation";
- To accumulate specific savings;
- To reduce your mortgage by a specific amount;
- To eliminate or reduce borrowing;
- **Not committing** to spend funds before you receive them.

These goals should be congruent with your **Life Goals**.

When to Prepare a Budget and How Far Ahead

When do you prepare the budget? The answer is obvious—before the event. However, individuals tend to wait until they start their journey. Strive always to complete the budget ahead of the trip. That's when you have all options!

How long should be the budgeting period? For the duration of the "journey"; typically one year for the normal household budget. The period must cover a full cycle of spending; if you are at school, it should span the school year.

Another relevant question is this: "How do I divide the expenses for the year?" Although individuals receive salaries weekly or bi-weekly, they allocate amounts monthly, for one year ahead. Select the period and increment (weekly, bi-weekly, or monthly) with which you are comfortable.

Essential Information to Prepare a Budget

Before starting the budgeting process, understand your spending pattern. Analyze expenditures over the past six months. Use relevant expense categories (such as groceries, entertainment, and so on) that you select. Separate categories into discretionary[3] and non-discretionary. Thereafter, start recording your spending (shortly I will mention the relevant forms) using these categories. You will need six to nine months to grasp your expenditure pattern.

Life Goals are crucial to the budget preparation process. They help you develop specific goals for the budgeting period. So too is your cash flow statement. Review cash flows for the previous six to twelve months. Use the knowledge gained to compute estimated income and expenses for the next twelve months.

What if you have not budgeted before? Probably you do not have a cash flow statement. Like many people, you won't know your current spending pattern!

Figure 2 shows an example of the spending pattern of the average Canadian family taken from the 1996 Census. Persons budgeting for the first time may find this useful. Naturally, your lifestyle will determine your expenditure pattern.

Other information you will need to prepare your budget includes the following:

- Details of loans and other commitments;
- Pay slips to guide you about income details;

- Insurance policies to get premium information;
- Housing details—mortgage and property taxes;
- Special repairs or purchases;
- Car manual to try to estimate likely service requirements;
- Other....

Probably your first budget will show estimated expenditures at twice your income! Don't be surprised by this initial result! Likewise, you will be amazed at the size of your prior spending level.

Figure 2: Household Expenditures Canada Wide (Average Income $51,000)[4]

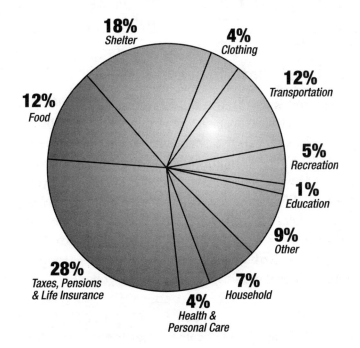

PEACE Budgetary Computation Forms (PBCF)

Now I turn to the budget preparation forms. I will examine the **PEACE** Budgetary Computation Forms in Appendix II, which I recommend for those preparing their initial budget. Although I show two forms, one for income and another for expenses, I will consider them as two sections of one form in my review.

The top section of the PBCF, where I show selected goals, is key: I list relevant **Life Goals** and other specific goals to be achieved during the budget period. This section helps to focus your estimates.

Use one of the many computer software programs available, if possible. If you are inexperienced at budgeting and are uncomfortable with the computer, start with the manual form. Both the manual and computer system use similar principles, but the computer package will be more flexible.

Source of Data For the PBCF

We get most of the data to prepare the **PBCF** from the cash flow statement in Table IV.[5] The **PBCF** has three columns for the frequency of income and expenses. Record your estimated income and expenditure in the column that is appropriate—weekly, monthly, or yearly.

The **PBCF** form shows gross monthly salary at $3150, from which **you deduct your giving first**—before taxes and other payroll deductions! Develop this mindset of giving first, even before the government takes its share from your paycheque! To complete the income section, deduct **Savings** (the example in Appendix 2 excludes Savings) and **Capital Fund** amounts from gross income. Then determine the net balance to allocate to the various expense categories. This example reflects $1800 available for allocation.

After recording all income and expense items you expect to occur during the budget period, compute the monthly budget amounts in the "Monthly Budget" column by multiplying weekly amounts by four, and dividing yearly amounts by twelve.

Four Important Budget Items on the PBCF

Additional to goals during the planning period, every completed **PBCF** should include at least four key components—the first three in the **income** section and the fourth in the **expense** section:

- **Giving**
- **Savings**
- **Capital Fund**
- **Contingency**

Giving

Giving is first. Often we think of giving as a tithe or one tenth of our income only. However, if truly we accept the **GAS** Principle—which states, inter alia, that we are mere managers of God's money—we must spend effectively, 100% of gross income. Consequently, we ought to change our mind-set to this: Recognize that 100% of all income is God's, maximize giving and minimize the amount we keep. This is out-of-the-box thinking - a reversal of our normal thinking!

Genesis 14:20 records the first incidence of tithing in the Bible. It was voluntary, done out of gratitude and as a part of Abraham's worship to God following his rescue of Lot: three essential elements of giving to the Lord.

Under Mosaic law, the Israelites were **required** to give at least 23% in three different tithes:

- **The Festive Tithe** was consumed by the giver (Deuteronomy 14:22-23).
- **The Levite Tithe** - *"... as their inheritance in return for the work they do while serving at the Tent of Meeting..."* (Numbers 18: 21-24).
- **The Poor Tithe** (Every three years) - Deuteronomy 14:28-29 - *"... bring all the tithes of that year's produce and store it in your towns, so that the Levites (who have no allotment or inheritance of their own) and the aliens, the fatherless and the widows who live in your towns may come and eat and be satisfied...."*

Further, kings often demanded **Tithes** as a form of taxation (1 Samuel 8:15-17) and **Gleanings** were to be left for the poor - *"... do not reap to the very edges of your field or gather the gleanings of your harvest..."* (Leviticus 19:9-10).

Proverbs 3:9 **(NIV)** tells us to *"Honour the Lord with your wealth, with the first fruits of all your crops"*. God first! Apostle Paul in 2 Corinthians 9:7 states:

Each man should give what he has decided in his heart to give, not reluctantly or under compulsion, for God loves a cheerful giver. And God is able to make all grace abound to you, so that in all things at all times, having all that you need, you will abound in every good work.

This is hilarious giving: not under duress, not out of guilt, but under God's direction following prayer. As Christians we are obliged to fund the great commission in Matthew 28:18-20. We are to *"...make disciples of all nations...."* This needs funding. We must give first to our local church then to other Christian organizations. Let us become like the Macedonians who gave themselves first then gave as much as they were able... and beyond their ability. Read what Paul says in 2 Corinthians 8:1-7 **(NIV):**

> *[1]And now, brothers, we want you to know about the grace that God has given the Macedonian churches. [2]Out of the most severe trial, their overflowing joy and their extreme poverty welled up in rich generosity. [3]For I testify that they gave as much as they were able, and even beyond their ability. Entirely on their own, [4]they urgently pleaded with us for the privilege of sharing in this service to the saints. [5]And they did not do as we expected, but they gave themselves first to the Lord and then to us in keeping with God's will.... [7]But just as you excel in everything—in faith, in speech, in knowledge, in complete earnestness and in your love for us—see that you also excel in this grace of giving.*

Focus on maximising your giving as a part of worship to the Lord! Since God owns everything, the key question to answer is this: How much should I keep? Minimize this amount.

Hold recipients accountable. Where there is blatant, unrepentant abuse of donated funds by a receiving church or other organization, redirect giving until the situation is rectified.

Savings

Savings are second. Genesis 40 and 41 portray an excellent biblical example of respect for God and saving for a future event. God revealed to Pharaoh in a dream that there would be seven years of abundance followed by seven years of famine in Egypt. Because Joseph explained the dream, Pharaoh put him in charge of Egypt to implement God's plan. **For seven years, Joseph systematically stored excess food.** Over the next seven years of drought, Egypt had enough food!

Learn to save regularly, at least 3-5% of gross salary from each salary cheque. This is additional to contributions to your Registered Retirement Savings Plan (RRSP[6]) and to your company's registered pension plan. Abide by these guidelines:

- Do not use regular savings (this 3-5%) to supplement your household budget.

- Maximize your annual pension and RRSP contributions.

- Consider regular savings as payroll deductions. Indeed arrange for automatic transfer to your bank, if possible.

Later, regular savings will provide the base for prudent investing.

Here is a modern day example of **giving, saving,** and control of money to emulate.

Oseola McCarty,[7] 87, did one thing all her life: laundry. Now she's famous for it—or at least for what she did with $150,000 of the $250,000 she saved by washing the dirty clothes of wealthy bankers and merchants in her hometown of Hattiesburg, Mississippi. For decades she earned 50 cents per load (a week's worth of one family's laundry). But when she finally laid down her old-fashioned washboard—which she always preferred over new-fangled electric washing machines—McCarty decided to ask her banker how much money she had stowed away.

The figure astounded her. Then it set her to thinking. "I had more than what I could use in the bank," she explained to Christian Reader, "and I can't carry anything away from here with me, so I thought it was best to give it to some child to get an education."

To the astonishment of school officials, the soft-spoken, never-married laundry woman from a not-so-posh part of town gave $150,000 to the nearby University of Southern Mississippi to help African-American young people attend college. The first recipient is 18-year-old Stephanie Bullock, a freshman at USM, who has already invited Miss McCarty to her 1999 graduation ceremony.

To date, McCarty has been interviewed by Barbara Walters, each of the major network news programs, CNN, People magazine... and the list goes on. Though she had never traveled out of the South before, McCarty visited the White House, where President Clinton awarded her the Presidential Citizenship Award.

McCarty attends Friendship Baptist Church and reads her Bible every morning and prays on her knees every evening. Discounting the publicity, she says she is simply grateful for the chance to help others gain what she lost: in the sixth grade she was pulled out of school to care for an ailing family member and to help her mother with the laundry.

"It's more blessed to give than to receive," she

tells reporters when they ask why she didn't use the money on herself. "I've tried it."

Capital Fund: The Way to Accumulate Funds For Large Expenses

Companies accumulate funds from current income to replace assets (buildings, machines, etc.) that they employ to earn that income. We call this **depreciation**. For a machine that costs $1000 with a life of 10 years, a company may set aside $100 each year to replace it in 10 years. The alternative would be to wait and hope that the company will have funds at replacement time, which is not practical.

Usually individuals do not plan to purchase cars, refrigerators, stoves, carpets, heat pumps, and other major equipment. They buy them as needed and often they use credit. Similarly, when they need to repair or replace these items, they use funds from the household budget, which means they must forego some other expense item. Generally, they borrow. This ad hoc asset replacement and asset maintenance can be stressful and expensive.

I suggest that all individuals and couples copy corporations and systematically provide for replacing and repairing capital equipment. Accordingly, accumulate funds systematically in a **Capital Fund** to finance major purchases and large maintenance expenses. Implementing this will eliminate crises from your annual budgets. Here are examples of expenditures that the **Capital Fund** should cover:

- Down payment on a home
- Purchase of a car

- Purchase of major furniture and appliances for the home
- Children's education
- Repairs and renovation to the home
- Repairs of the car and appliances
- Other major purchases

Individuals and couples who attend my seminars and whom I have counselled testify repeatedly that the **Capital Fund** had the greatest positive impact on their finances. You need a **Capital Fund** to become and to remain **debt-free**. Ultimately, you can plan your major purchases for which you will pay cash. You will pay cash also from the **Capital Fund** for unplanned repairs and maintenance expenses as they occur.

Ideally, start a **Capital Fund** in your early teens. Therefore, encourage your teenagers to start their **Fund** now, contributing regularly at least 50% of all income received (I will elaborate later in the final chapter of this section).

Allocate at least 5% of your gross income to your **Capital Fund**. Initially, the exact percentage is not critical; development of habitual contribution to the **Fund is key**.

At your next salary increase, and whenever you get unexpected funds, place them in your **Capital Fund**. Continue saving your net salary increase for at least twelve months. Keep building this account until the **Fund** is large enough to meet relevant planned and unexpected expenses listed above. Thereafter, as the **Fund** grows, you will develop a base for more "aggressive" giving and prudent investing.

Where should you keep the **Capital Fund?** In a savings account? On fixed deposit? It depends on the size of the **Fund**! Initially, place your deposits where you can access them quickly, like a money market account.[8] As it grows, use other short-term investment vehicles. Consult an independent financial adviser to guide you. However, do not buy stocks or bonds, which are long-term investment instruments. **The Capital Fund** deposits are additional to your savings and your contingency budget.

It is never too late to start a **Capital Fund**. Start today so you will not borrow to replace and repair your major assets!

Contingency

Do not confuse a **Contingency** with the **Capital Fund**. You need the **Contingency** until you know your spending pattern and become comfortable with budgeting. The **Contingency budget** will provide funds for major unplanned expenses, until you have an established **Capital Fund**.[9]

Your initial budget may exclude inadvertently certain items such as insurance premiums, loan payments or hair care expenses. You would pay these items from the contingency budget. The less experienced you are at budgeting and recording your spending, the larger should be the contingency. Initially, allocate 10% of your gross income until you become familiar with your spending pattern. Reduce this percent to 5% or less thereafter.

Finalizing the Budget

Don't be surprised if, when you finish allocating budgeted amounts, your total expenses represent twice your available income; a common first budget result. Now the fun begins as you start the inevitable "cutting" exercise! **Before finalizing the budget, go exploring!** Review the following areas and you may find available funds:

- Cable/Telephone/Internet charges
- Entertainment/Eating out/Daily Lunch Expenses
- Bank Charges/Credit Card Interest
- Insurance Premiums
- Car Lease Payments
- Gifts
- Vacation Expenses

Use the same review process here as I will discuss in the following chapter under the heading, **"Three Aids to Apply to Major Spending Decisions."** During your re-examination, remember this quote from Benjamin Franklin: "Beware of little expenses: a small leak will sink a great ship." [10]

One couple found $150 per month in the above categories as they explored! Your major challenge will be separating categories into "wants" and "needs," and "cutting" some needs!

Before closing this chapter, I would like to share with you a few **budget truisms** that I can confirm.

Budget Truisms

- You will **never have enough money** unless you **control your spending!**
- Your expenses will increase as your income increases, unless you **control your spending.**
- More money is not usually the answer to financial

problems: **changed attitudes and behaviour** are the major steps.

Think About This

If you do not pay your credit card balance in full monthly, you cannot afford to keep a credit card!

Chapter Notes:

[1] You may not have to borrow from a third party. However, you would "borrow" funds that should be available for other areas.

[2] Today the Canadian Federal budget is in surplus (income exceeds expenses). Budgets of several Provincial Governments also are in surplus. The Federal Finance Minister estimates that over the next five years (starting in 2000), the Federal budget will generate about $100 billion of surplus. Yet, only five years ago, all levels of governments were saddled with large deficits! Low interest rates and strong economies helped to reduce the surplus, but in my opinion, the single most important fact was a determination by each government to focus its efforts on eliminating the surplus. You, too, must make elimination of budget deficits a top priority. I have noticed throughout my career that when we make an item a priority for action, benefits ensue.

[3] Discretionary items such as "entertainment" and "cable TV charges" are items for which you have an option to spend or not to spend.

[4] *Statistics Canada*, 96 Census.

[5] See "Essential Information Needed to Prepare a Budget" that I discussed earlier in this chapter.

[6] An RRSP allows you to save income earned today and get

a tax deduction on the amount saved (there is a limit). Income earned in the RRSP account is tax-free until it is withdrawn. In theory, you will withdraw amounts when you retire. Refer to Section III for further discussions on RRSPs.

[7] Kevin Dale Miller, "Ordinary Heroes," *Christian Reader*, March/April 1996, p. 81.

[8] A money market account is a safe and accessible account that you can operate with a financial institution. Funds in this account are invested predominantly in Treasury Bills (Loans to the Government). The interest rate that you earn is higher than on regular bank deposits. Generally, you need to give 48 hours' notice to withdraw the funds.

[9] A Capital Fund is "established" when you no longer need to use funds from your routine household budget for major purchases or repairs.

[10] Bob Phillips, *Phillips' Book of Great Thoughts and Funny Sayings* (Wheaton, IL: Tyndale House Publishers, Inc., 1993), p. 117.

7

The Control Phase of PEACE
(Act, Compare, and Execute)

Having completed the **budgeting phase (Planning and Estimating)** of the **PEACE** system, we move to the **control** phase which includes three steps:

- **Acting** on plans made and recording the actual result;
- **Comparing** what you did with what you planned to do;
- **Executing** any changes necessary.

Let's examine the first step, **Acting** on plans and recording the actual result. It entails the following:

- Establishing accountability
- Choosing a bank account(s)

- Recording your spending
- Recording progress toward achieving goals
- Implementing three spending aids: The **GAS** principle, the **PLANE** Spending Analysis and the **Affordability Index**

Establishing Accountability

Before starting the **control** phase, establish accountability to implement and to follow the **PEACE** system. Accountability is entrenched in many successful businesses. It is answering to someone for your actions. Usually governments and individuals do not practice it. As Christians we are accountable as follows:

- To Jesus Christ for the stewardship of His resources (Matthew 25:14-30);
- To our brothers and sisters in Christ (Galatians 6:2) to help us stay focussed on a goal or goals, and to encourage one another (support groups play this role).

Choose someone trustworthy with whom you feel comfortable. You don't need to give him all the details of your affairs. Give him the right to ask a simple question: "Have you been following the **PEACE** system?" Remember, you are spending God's money, and you are accountable to Jesus!

Choosing a Bank Account

What's the big deal with a bank account? No two bank accounts are alike. Have you reviewed options that banks offer recently? In September 1999, I did. I collected booklets from major Canadian banks about their service fees. At least one of these booklets has over twenty pages explaining different accounts and services with related costs! The conditions attached to each vary, and some accounts are costly to operate.

First, determine your banking needs: the number of cheques you write monthly and the number of accounts needed (**Capital Fund,** savings, and regular chequing). If you operate a manual system, use two accounts. With a computer system, if uncomfortable with one account, try two. Into one account deposit your salary, to the other your estimated month's spending. Transfer amounts monthly.

Before finalizing your banking arrangements, shop around to evaluate different accounts. Select the appropriate account, choosing consciously between an account with a bank or with a credit union.[1] Pick one or two accounts that fit your needs, at a reasonable cost. I have seen individuals pay over $20 per month of bank charges besides ATM fees, for no special services!

Recording Your Spending: The PEACE Budget Worksheet (PBW)

Now decide how to record your actual spending. As I said before, if this is your first budget, you may wish to use a manual form. In Appendix III, I show a form that I see many people use—the **PEACE** Budget Worksheet ("PBW"). I have over twenty different forms that I have used with various persons: I attach three samples as Appendices III-1, 2, and 3.

Examine the many computer software programs available and, if comfortable, use an appropriate one. Usually they are simple and have user manuals to guide you. Some programs are sophisticated and include several features to perform, among others, the following tasks:

- Processing many currencies,
- Operating more than one budget,
- Handling investments.

To continue our discussions, however, I will comment on the **PBW,** as the principles for manual and computer packages are similar.

Before spending, transfer **monthly budgeted amounts** from the **PBCF** in Appendix II to the appropriate section of the **PBW**. This **PBW** helps you calculate balances left in each budget category. After spending any amount, whether by cash, cheque, or credit card, enter on the **PBW** the following:

- Date of the transaction;
- Description of expense and/or the name of the supplier;
- Amount (indicating, if necessary, whether cash, cheque, or credit card);
- Balance left for that budget category.

Many people state that it is inconvenient to complete the **PCW** after each transaction. Therefore, **reserve two to three hours weekly** to do the following, as appropriate:

- Recording and reviewing actual expenses;
- Reconciling bank and credit statements;
- Comparing actual and planned spending;
- Comparing progress toward your goal(s) with the plan;

- Deciding if changes will be necessary to accomplish goals.

Instead of using the **PBW**, you may consider applying the system my mother used! The tried and proven **Envelope** System! It is simple! Place cash in an envelope marked with the name of the budget category and spend the cash from that envelope. When the envelope is empty, the budget is finished for that item!

My wife, Doreen, uses a variation of the **Envelope** System for the portion of our family budget that she administers. On each envelope, she writes the budget amount, details of spending, and balance left. In the envelope, she inserts credit card receipts and other relevant bills for that budget category. This works for her. She does not put cash in envelopes. For the section of the budget that I operate, I use a computer software package.

In our home, we have one budget divided into two parts. Every budget item has an "owner," Doreen or me. For each budget category, one of us is responsible to ensure that we stay on track or to signal early that we will have a problem, so we may take corrective action. This is one of our budget principles. During our early married years, life was simple, expense categories were few, and this principle was not necessary. However, as our finances became complex, we adopted the present approach. I emphasize, however, that we have one budget which we manage jointly by allocating specific budget categories to each of us.

We allocate "ownership" of each category based on convenience. Nevertheless, together we prepare the budget and together we review it regularly. I record total spending using a computer software package. Doreen uses the **PBW** manual form to record her spending details.

She operates two bank accounts: the Budget Smoothing Account ("**BSA**") for household expenditures, car insurance, education, gifts, her clothing, and other items she "controls;" and the Regular Chequing Account ("**RCA**") into which she transfers the current month's estimated cash expenses. Into the **BSA**, she deposits the total monthly allocation. Into the **RCA**, she transfers from the **BSA** cash she will spend in the month. If car insurance premiums were $1200 for the year, monthly she would deposit $100 into the **BSA**. When we receive the insurance premium invoice, she will transfer $1200 from the **BSA** into the **RCA**. She does likewise for similar expenses.

Choose the method with which you are comfortable. For couples, remember you must decide who will record actual spending. It's confusing if both record at different times!

Recording Progress Toward Achieving Goals

Keep a dedicated notebook or computer file to record your goals (both **Life Goals** and budget goals) and the steps necessary to achieve them. These are not necessarily financial. You may decide to do a second degree within a certain time frame. Identify intermediary targets. Track your progress toward your goals regularly when you review your spending.

Systematically review and record progress toward your **Life Goals**. Because these tend to be long-term, it is easy to defer them. Don't! Remember today is yesterday's tomorrow! Take one step closer to that **Life Goal** today.

If you have a budget goal to repay credit card debts fully during the budget period, note the progress at each review session:

- Amount paid to date compared with plan;
- Amount unpaid compared with plan.

Implementing Three Spending Aids

Now you are ready to **Act**! Before any major commitment of funds and before you decide to include a significant expense in your budget, apply these three spending aids. They are your prime control mechanism in the **control** phase of the **PEACE** system:

- The **GAS** Principle
- The **PLANE** Spending Analysis
- The **Affordability Index**

I will expand on each of the above in Chapter 8. Meanwhile, let's move to the next step in the process, **comparing** what you did with what you planned to do.

Comparing What You Did With What You Planned to Do

In the **PEACE** system, every segment is essential. Often we neglect this **Comparing** step. Initially, many persons complain that it is cumbersome and time consuming. I agree! Usually they reverse this view after a couple months.

Comparing actual results with planned results is vital to the **PEACE** budgetary control system! It's an early warning routine! Its objective is **to signal early** potential problems with achieving your goal so that you may **take action quickly** to avert any deviation from the plan. I will address the following issues briefly:

- When to do the comparison
- How to do it
- Who should do it

When to Do the Comparison

For a regular monthly budget, I suggested earlier that you set aside two to three hours weekly to do this comparison among other things. Stick to a weekly routine, otherwise you will ignore this critical step. With ad hoc comparisons, you lose some options to correct deviations.

Try to use the same location each week. Ensure that you have all the necessary information at each session. Hang on to your chair! Don't laugh! Try to make this fun! Yes, fun! Why not go on a weekly date after you and your spouse finish the exercise?

How to Do This Comparison

Your goal at this step is to answer two questions:

- How does my actual progress toward achieving my goal compare with my planned progress? You would have provided most of the answers to this question in the earlier section called, "**Recording Progress Toward Achieving Goals.**"
- How much have I spent to achieve my actual progress to date compared with the corresponding budget?

Unless you spent time at the budgeting stage identifying measurement factors, the process will be cumbersome, time consuming, and frustrating. In management we say, "If you can't measure it, you can't manage it!" This applies to our personal lives, too. If you do not identify in advance measurable interim targets, you won't know how you are doing during your journey!

In your Vancouver trip example, you decided to stop in Regina. The estimated cost up to Regina would be a measurement factor. When you reached Regina, you would compare actual cost with this estimate.

For your monthly budget, dollar costs per category would be your measurement factor. Review all measurement factors and compare with your actual expenses. Suppose you planned to take a vacation in September at a cost of $2400. You would decide to reserve $200 per month for this item. In April, one of your measurement factors would be $800 (4 x $200) reserved for this vacation.

Make comparisons on a year-to-date basis. You may be within budget one month but over another. Further, at this comparison session, look ahead to determine whether you will have enough resources for the rest of the year or the rest of the journey.

Before finishing the session, ensure you answered the two questions I mentioned above. Identify clearly the reasons for each deviation from plan. Here, computer software packages offer a great advantage: They provide flexibility for various analyses and comparisons quickly and easily.

Who Should Do the Comparison?

For couples, both husband and wife should be involved. Both must be committed to the process and both should have knowledge of progress. Initially, reward yourself with a small treat each time you do this exercise!

Executing Changes to Remain on Course to Achieve Your Plan

What happens if the results of the budget comparison show that you are off target? First, you review your goals to ensure that they are still relevant. Next, you determine what options exist to get back on track. Then you select one of them.

Except when you use the **Affordability Index**[2] to evaluate your major expenditures, I do not endorse shifting funds within the budget to cover overspending on **discretionary** items. Don't transfer funds from one under-spent **discretionary** category (vacation expenses) to an over-spent **discretionary** category (entertainment). However, you may transfer amounts to cover an overspent **non-discretionary** item (groceries). Of course, I apply this guideline only after your budget gestation period (no more than six month) is over! In the initial phase, do what you must to understand your spending pattern.

What if, in September, you notice that for the year you might overspend two **non-discretionary** items, **groceries** and **gasoline**? Examine your options! You may find sufficient funds in **discretionary** budgets of **gifts**, **entertainment**, and **meals**. **Reallocate funds from these categories to the two non-discretionary items (groceries and gasoline).** You would not do the reverse, however—take funds from **groceries** to **entertainment**!

For your monthly budget, the journey ends only on December 31. Then on January 1, it restarts. **Executing** changes is not the end of the process. It may be the start!

Examine all aspects of the **PEACE** Budgetary Control System, and remember, it never stops! Amend any part that becomes irrelevant or that needs changing. As a reminder, I will reproduce Figure 1 here.

Figure 1: The PEACE Budgetary Control System

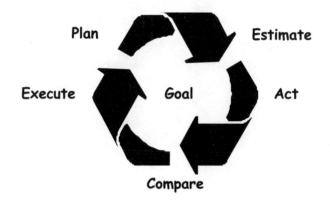

Think About This

*Since today is yesterday's tomorrow, putting off starting the **PEACE** Budgetary Control System to tomorrow is futile! Start today!*

Chapter Notes:

[1] A Credit Union is a financial institution in which the depositors own the institution.

[2] Refer to Chapter 8 for a full discussion of the Affordability Index.

8

The Control Phase of PEACE
(Implementing Three Spending Aids)

The **GAS** Principle
The **PLANE** Spending Analysis
The **Affordability** Index

Before committing to major expenditures[1] (you decide what's major—I have seen as low as $50 per transaction), apply these three spending aids. They are your prime control mechanisms in the **control** phase of the **PEACE** system:

- The **GAS** Principle ("**GAS**")
- The **PLANE** Spending Analysis ("**PLANE**")
- The **Affordability Index**

I explained in Section I that **GAS** was the foundation of the **PEACE** Budgetary Control System. I indicated that it was essential to manage God's money effectively. Before I explain its application, here is a recap:

The GAS Principle

Key Truth #1: **G**od Owns Everything (Psalm 24:1, Colossians 1:16)

Key Truth #2: **A**ccept What You Have (1 Timothy 6:7-8, Hebrews 13:5)

Key Truth #3: **S**eek First His Kingdom and Submit Your Requests to Him (Matthew 6:33, Proverbs 19:21)

To apply **GAS** to your proposed expenses, ask the questions below **before** you **commit** to spend.

Application of Key Truth #1: (God Owns Everything)

- Will the spending decision directly or indirectly **conflict** with Jesus' teaching in the Bible?
- Will it **promote** or **condone** abortion, hate, greed, lust, or sexual immorality?

This is Apostle Paul's comment on the matter:

Do you not know that wrongdoers will not inherit the kingdom of God? Do not be deceived! Fornicators, idolaters, adulterers, male prostitutes, sodomites, thieves, the greedy, drunkards, revilers, robbers— none of these will inherit the kingdom of God.[2]

I call these questions the **external** drivers of **GAS**. They focus on the **nature** of expenditures. I am not suggesting that you become paranoid trying to trace the final sources of all your spending! I am reminding you that it's God's money you are managing, not yours. Consequently, you should not knowingly spend funds that ultimately will dishonour Jesus. Your spending must reflect your beliefs as a Christian!

Application of Key Truth #2: (Accept What You Have)

- Am I being selfish?
- Am I being greedy?
- Am I just keeping up with the Jones?

This is Jesus' remark:

And he said to them, "Take care! Be on your guard against all kinds of greed; for one's life does not consist in the abundance of possessions." [3]

These are the **internal** drivers. They focus on **you** and your **motives**. Even if the contemplated expenditure honours Christ (more accurately, it does not dishonour Him), you must examine your heart and understand your motives for spending. Another helpful question is this: Am I accumulating things that are nice to have but not necessary?

Application of Key Truth #3: (Seek First His Kingdom and Submit Your Requests to Him)

- How is my walk with God?
- Have I been feeding on His Word?

• Have I prayed and sought to know God's will?

Here is Apostle Paul again:

Do not be conformed to this world, but be transformed by the renewing of your minds, so that you may discern what is the will of God—what is good and acceptable and perfect.[4]

These are the **eternal** drivers. They are the bottom line! They focus on your walk.

I mentioned in the introduction to this book that the Bible does not promise you material riches if you do God's will. It promises blessings! You will know the form of blessings only when you receive them! That's good enough for me; how about you?

I encourage you to reflect on **GAS**. Sure, it requires effort and time. I assure you that if you decide to walk with Jesus and live a holy life, it is merely one aspect of such a life. You could say that I work in finance, thus I am quite comfortable and accustomed to analyzing spending decisions. You would be correct! But **GAS** is not about financial analysis; it is stewardship in action!

PLANE Spending Analysis

Why do we need another set of questions? Why isn't **GAS** adequate? The **PLANE** analysis complements the **GAS** principle; use them sequentially. If the result of the **GAS** analysis is negative, do not proceed to the **PLANE**. "Do not pass go, do not collect $200!"

The first two sets of questions of **GAS** focus on **external** and **internal** drivers; they are concerned with **what** and **why**. The **PLANE** analysis, on the other hand, goes further and deals with the following:

- **Why Now**—Did you plan it?
- **How**—How will you pay for it?
- **Alternatives**—Are there alternatives available?
- **Necessity**—Do I truly need it?
- **Effectiveness**—Is this the most effective use of God's resources now?

The third set of questions (the third Key Truth) from **GAS** applies equally to the **PLANE** analysis. Indeed, think of PLANES! If followed systematically, the **PLANE** and the **Affordability Index** will keep you out of debt. Here are the **PLANE** questions:

P Did I **Plan** this expenditure and did I include it in my budget?

L Will the expenditure increase my **Loans**?

A Are there realistic **Alternatives** to achieve my spending objective?

N Is the expenditure **Necessary** to achieve my spending objective?

E Is this the most **Effective** use of resources now, relative to my **Life Goals** and **budget goals?**

Before explaining each question and discussing the related spending aid, the **Affordability Index**, I will repeat four key definitions from Chapter 5:

- A **Goal** is your **destination**—where you wish to go.

- A **Plan** is your **journey**—the steps to achieve your goal.

- An **Estimate** is the likely cost of the **plan**—the cost of the steps in the **plan**.

- A **Budget** is a record of the results of the **planning and estimating** processes.

Underpinning the **PLANE** analysis is this: Every spending decision has a **basic objective** that you should identify in your evaluation. If you decide to buy a new bicycle, you should know the reason for the purchase. Is it to enter a special race during the summer, for outdoor exercise, or for a different reason? For the discussions in this chapter, let's assume that the spending objective is to enter a bicycle race during the summer.

I will discuss each question of the **PLANE** analysis in detail when I examine the **Affordability Index.** Now I wish to discuss key aspects only of each question:

Plan

The **PEACE** system is predicated on **the following:**

Goals (your destination—trip to Vancouver) that translate into...

   plans (how you will get there), the cost of which you...

      estimate to become...

         budget allocations ($300 for transportation, accommodation, meals, etc.).

If you change your **goal** (cancel your Vancouver trip), you automatically cancel your **plan** because it becomes irrelevant. **Accordingly**, the original **budget** allocation ($300 allocation for that trip) will be frozen automatically and must not be spent without further discussion and analysis. I apply this principle to all **specific, discretionary items**,[5] but not to non-discretionary items such as groceries and laundry.

Loans

This includes all forms of loans: from bankers, department stores, lay-away plans, and so on. Unless you pay your credit card balance in full, your loans will increase when you use your card. Further, it does not matter that you planned the expenditure and included it in your budget.

Alternative

Identify **realistic** alternatives only. Focus on alternative ways to achieve the spending objective.

Necessary

We can go to extremes and define "necessary" to either include or exclude most purchases. In this context, an item is **necessary if it satisfies the predefined spending objective** (a bicycle to enter a bicycle race in the summer). Thus, in this section of the analysis, we focus on the appropriateness of the item for the spending objective only (is this the best bicycle to use in the race?).

We do not challenge the spending objective (the need to enter a bicycle race) because we would have dealt with that issue when we applied **GAS** to this proposed decision. In applying the external, internal, and eternal drivers that we discussed earlier, we would have established the need for the item. The **Affordability Index** helps us to decide if we can afford the item! We may not be able to afford the item even if it is necessary!

Effective

Unlike the other questions, we evaluate effectiveness based on **Life Goals** and **budget goals**, not on spending objectives. This approach ensures that we focus on the bigger picture!

Assume that your most pressing **goal** is to reduce your loans, and now you wish to buy a discretionary item such as a portable cassette player. Would buying this item be the most effective use of resources now? No, because it would conflict with your **goal** for the budget period—to reduce your loans.

The Affordability Index

I designed the **Affordability Index** after using the **PLANE** analysis alone for a couple years. I had a problem with the subjective results of the **PLANE** when I compared two or more spending decisions; thus, I decided to quantify the answers. When answering "Plan," "Loans," "Alternative," and "Necessary" questions for the Affordability Index, the spending objective is critical.

Below are the questions to answer as you complete the **Affordability Index.** Also below is the process you would follow to decide if you should buy the bicycle to enter a bicycle race during the summer. Review these comments in conjunction with Table V on page 111.

Plan

In or Can Be Accommodated	0
Out and Cannot Be Accommodated	2

If you change your **plan** to buy a specific item, the original budget allocated for that item is frozen automatically. However, it is available to "accommodate" purchasing an item to which you apply the **Affordability Index**. For example, if you **planned** to buy a CD player and included $150 in the **budget**, this amount is available for a CD player **only**! If you are not going to buy the CD player, this $150 is **frozen and not available** for any other item, although it was in the budget. You changed your plans; the money is **not available** in the budget!

However, now you wish to buy a bicycle for $150, which you excluded from both your plan and your budget. It can be "accommodated" in the plan (because you will no longer buy the CD player) provided your total actual expenses for the budget period will not exceed your total budgeted expenses for that period. For example, if your budget for the year was $20,000 and you estimate now that you will spend less than that— $19,850—you may accommodate the purchase. Otherwise, you may not.

- If the bicycle was in the plan, score **zero**.[6] Also if it was not in the plan but can be accommodated as in our example above, score **zero**. Otherwise, score **two**.

Loans

Unchanged	0
Increase	6

To buy this bicycle, will your **loans** increase? Score **zero** if your loans will not increase and **six** if they will. It does not matter if it is in the budget! The test here is based strictly on the change in your total loans, including credit card purchases. **A credit card charge will score a six unless you have sufficient funds in your bank account to cover the charge, and you plan to pay the balance in full when due.** The PEACE system teaches you to strive to be debt-free. The **Affordability Index** captures this and penalizes all borrowing. I will discuss one exception later—purchasing a car that you need to earn your living.

Alternative

None	0
Yes	2

Is there a realistic **alternative** to achieve the **spending objective**? Not necessarily an alternative bicycle, just an alternative to achieve the objective. If your objective were to enter a bicycle race, the viable alternative would be a different type of bicycle. If the objective were outdoor exercise, the realistic alternative could be walking or jogging depending on other factors. Do not be concerned with an alternative-spending objective. Score **two** for a realistic alternative and **zero** if none.

- Why do you score any points if there is a realistic alternative? Doesn't this penalize you? Sure, it does. If there is a realistic alternative, perform a separate analysis on the **Affordability Index** and compare results.

Necessary

Yes	0
No	4

Is the bicycle, or the alternative identified, **necessary** to achieve the **spending objective**? If your answer is yes, score **zero**; if no, score **four**.

Effective

Yes	0
No	6

For this fifth question, it is your **Life Goals** and **budget goals** that are relevant, **not the spending objective.** Is this the most effective use of resources relative to your **Life** and **budget goals** now? You may ask this question another way: Will this amount reduce the amount needed to achieve a **Life** or **budget goal**? For example, if a budget goal was to eliminate credit card balances, will this expense reduce cash available to achieve that goal? If it will not, score **zero**; if it will, score **six**. Apart from the **Vase** (which I will explain later), you can't "afford" an item on which spending is not the most effective use of resources!

Apart from two exceptions, you cannot **afford** an item if one or more of the following are true:

- If you have to **borrow** to buy it.
- If spending to buy it is not the most **effective** use of resources.
- If you did not **plan** the expenditure and it is not **necessary**.

Table V shows six different spending decisions, each with a different result. The microwave scored a perfect zero (you get the total score by adding the five highlighted answers). It was planned; it did not increase your loans; there were no practical alternatives to reheat quickly; it was necessary now; and this was the most effective use of resources now. The opposite was true for the boat.

I encourage you to try this **Index**[7] with specific examples. As I illustrated above, the scoring system is simple. The scores for a proposed purchase are shown in the highlighted box and either are zero or the specific numbers reflected. Nothing else! Zero is the best (you can afford to spend) and twenty is the worst (you can't afford to spend).

For a score of eight or less (generally, it is eight), I developed two exceptions that I will explain below: spending on a **Vase**[8] and, under special circumstances, buying a car. I realize there is an element of subjectivity in this **Index**. Nevertheless, I think you will find it useful to evaluate major purchases. It is particularly helpful for comparing results of diverse analyses.

Table V: The Affordability Index

Spending Decisions	Micro Wave	Suit	University Course	Vase	Car	Boat
Objective Of Spending	Quick Reheat	Work	Self Improve-Ment	Specific Vacation	Work	Recreation
Plan						
In or Can Be Accommodated	0	0	0	0	0	0
Out and Cannot Be Accommodated	2	2	2	2	2	2
Loans						
Unchanged	0	0	0	0	0	0
Increase	6	6	6	6	6	6
Alternative						
None	0	0	0	0	0	0
Yes	2	2	2	2	2	2
Necessary						
Yes	0	0	0	0	0	0
No	4	4	4	4	4	4
Effective						
Yes	0	0	0	0	0	0
No	6	6	6	6	6	6
Total of Highlighted Numbers	0	4	4	8	8	20
Copyright © 1999, Michel A. Bell	←	Affordable	→	Special case	Special case	Not Affordable

Table VI: The Affordability Index Scoring Regime

SCORES	RESULTS
0—5	You **can** afford the item
6 & above (except for a Vase and a car)	You **can't** afford the item
8 or less	• You can afford the item as a **Vase**. • You **may** buy a **car** under specific circumstances.

The Affordability Index and the Vase

Several years ago, my wife introduced this concept into our planning and budgeting. She believed we were too inflexible in our allocations. She insisted that "we break a **Vase**" periodically and spend discretionary funds under specific conditions. She cited John 12:3-7 as the basis for the **Vase**:

> Mary took a pound of costly perfume made of pure nard, anointed Jesus' feet, and wiped them with her hair. The house was filled with the fragrance of the perfume. But Judas Iscariot, one of his disciples (the one who was about to betray him), said, "Why was this perfume not sold for three hundred denarii and the money given to the poor?" (He said this not because he cared about the poor, but because he was a thief; he kept the common purse and used to steal what was put into it.) Jesus said, "Leave her

alone. She bought it so that she might keep it for the day of my burial...."

Mary's sacrifice is key to this story. She chose to use this expensive perfume to anoint Jesus' feet instead of using it for herself. To include a **Vase** in your budget, you must be following strictly **GAS**, and its supporting cast of the **PEACE** system and **PLANE** analysis. Further, you must sacrifice!

To "break a **Vase,**" you would have scored eight or less on the **Affordability Index**, which would mean the following:

- The item is included **in the plan** and **in the budget initially.** Thus, the concept of **"not in the plan but can be accommodated" does not apply.** Accordingly, the expenditure must be agreed upon when you prepare the plan.
- Your **loans** will **not increase.**
- There **is** (usually) an **alternative.**
- The expense **is necessary** to achieve the spending objective.
- It **is not** the most **effective** use of resources.

This is the only instance that Doreen and I consider purchasing an item knowing that spending on that specific item is not the most effective use of resources at the time. Usually, therein lies the sacrifice; you forego achieving a **Life Goal** for a discretionary expenditure! Generally, a **Vase** applied to a special vacation that we have taken. When we went to Israel in 1989, we knew that we had to defer some specific goals.

We use these additional guidelines before we implement the **Vase**:

- I mentioned before that you must have been following rigorously the **GAS, PLANE,** and **PEACE** systems.
- We allow no more than one **Vase** per year (however, we do not implement one **Vase** every year).
- For a couple, each person must be in total agreement with all aspects of the decision.

The Affordability Index and the Purchase of a Car

Initially, I was not convinced that anyone should borrow to buy a car. However, Bill (my son-in-law) and Doreen convinced me, and after careful research, I added this exception. Scoring eight or less on the **Affordability Index** means also that you may purchase a car under certain conditions:

- You need the car to earn your living,
- There is no alternative,
- Your loans will increase, but
- This is the most effective use of resources.

Jonah graduated from University as an engineer. He has a job but there is no public transport to take him to work. A combination of a taxi and the bus during the week, and renting a car if needed on weekends would be cumbersome and expensive. **His only choice was to borrow money to buy a second-hand car.**

If you decide to buy a car with a loan,[9] you should adhere to the following guidelines:

- Don't buy a new car—you are likely to get the greatest value from a one to two-year-old car.
- Develop a plan to pay off the loan over a short period.
- Start the **GAS, PEACE, and PLANE** systems.
- Use the **Affordability Index** systematically.

Finally, in addition to the spending aids discussed above, you should try to develop specific habits to help you control your spending. Here are some tips:

Spending Tips

- **Do** remember that God provides always all the resources you **need**, which may be less than what you **want**!
- **Do** spend only when you know that spending is God's will for you. Ask the Lord to give you a verse of Scripture to confirm your "feelings." Before you spend, check the **PEACE Budget Worksheet** to see the allocation. If you have none left, maybe you can't spend.
  - Shop around before buying; visit second-hand stores.
  - Always read the fine print before signing any document.
  - If a "deal" seems too good to be true, **it is too good** to be true!
    - Why would a company give you a gift without strings? What's in it for them?
  - When you receive a raise or additional income, first allocate your tithe, then allocate the balance to the **Capital Fund**.

- Spend because there is a need!
- **Don't** spend impulsively.
  - When the urge comes, wait at least 24 to 48 hours and ensure that you apply the **GAS**, the **PLANE** and **Affordability Index**.
- **Don't** spend just because you have money.
- **Don't** go shopping **without** a list.
  - **Don't** buy anything that is not on the list.
  - **Don't** visit garage sales unless to buy specific budgeted items.
- **Don't** be enticed by **sales**.
  - You benefit from a sale only if you need the item you purchased. Seventy-five percent off is 25% too much if you do not need the item!
- **Don't** upgrade your home, your car, or "grown-up toys," unless you use the **GAS**, the **PLANE**, and the **Affordability Index**.
- **Don't** be embarrassed to negotiate prices.
- **Don't** use a credit card unless you have the funds in the bank.
  - A credit card is a cheque that is cleared in about thirty days.
  - If you can't pay your credit card balance in full every month, stop using it!
- **Don't** borrow except to buy a home—save for other items.
  - If you wish to borrow to maximize your RRSP contribution, you should repay the loan in full when you receive your tax refund. Otherwise, don't borrow.

Think About This

Control parameters provide boundaries that reduce stress and promote freedom!

Chapter Notes:

[1] Although I refer almost entirely to purchases of goods, the analyses refer equally to spending on services and other intangibles.

[2] 1 Corinthians 6:9-10

[3] Luke 12:15

[4] Romans 12:2

[5] Discretionary expense: An expense that you may decide not to incur, such as entertainment and a vacation.

[6] Highlight the box on the **Affordability Index** with the correct score.

[7] **The Affordability Index** (Copyright © May 1999, Michel A. Bell).

[8] A **Vase** is a purchase that scores eight or less on the **Affordability Index**, for which you must make a sacrifice.

[9] We will review the buy/lease decision in Section III.

9

Money Issues:
Couples and Children

Couples

In addition to the principles outlined earlier, persons intending to get married should discuss and agree on the guidelines they will apply to managing God's money. When I am negotiating a business partnership, I insist on goal congruence among the partners: ensuring that all parties share similar goals and values. Likewise, in a marriage relationship, you must confirm that both partners share the same values. Otherwise, you may find it difficult to agree on important issues. The Apostle Paul in 2 Corinthians 6:14 states it this way: *"Do not be mismatched with unbelievers. For what partnership is there between righteousness and lawlessness? Or what fellowship is there between light and darkness?"*

Goal congruence may not be difficult for the Christian couple seeking to serve the Lord. Their source of values will be the Bible. What if one person is a Christian and the other is not? If this state exists before marriage, they should not marry. If it happens after marriage, the Bible[1] states clearly that they must remain married, and by her lifestyle, the Christian may win over the non-Christian.

Here are some issues you should consider before you enter, and during, a marriage relationship:

- How do you set your **Life Goals** and **budget goals**? Refer to Chapter 3.

- How do you treat **assets that each brings into the marriage**? Do the assets enter one pool owned jointly or will they be separate? What about loans and other liabilities? Will they be assumed equally?

- How do you **title property** acquired after marriage? This is essential if the wife decides to be a stay-at-home mom to raise the children. I know men who refuse to acknowledge that a stay-at-home mom is an equal financial partner in the marriage! **My wife of thirty years has always been a stay-at-home mom, and I am proud of and indebted to her for the outstanding job she did raising our two children, now married.** Her job was made more challenging because of my many absences from home on overseas business trips. We title all properties in both our names. Examine your situation and get advice from a Christian perspective about your specific circumstances.

As you consider the previous two bullets, I urge you to meditate on the significance of **Genesis 2:24:** "Therefore a man leaves his father and his mother and clings to his wife, and they become one flesh." What does one flesh mean to you?

- What process or processes will you follow to decide on **major purchases**, such as buying a house or a car? What criteria do you use to decide between owning versus renting a home? What happens if you can't agree on a common result?
  - Surrender all decisions to Christ.
  - Pray and seek to know God's will.
  - Strive for unanimity always.

- Commit to starting and maintaining a **Capital Fund** from which you make all major purchases apart from monthly mortgage payments on your principal residence. Refer to Chapter 6.

- What is your attitude towards **borrowing?** Refer to Chapter 4.
  - Aim to be debt-free.
  - Borrow to buy your principal residence only.
  - Save for all other purchases.

- What about your children's and your individual **education expenses**? When and how do you save?

- Do you have a common view about entertaining and **eating out**?

  This is an area where I see couples struggle. One prefers eating out frequently, the other rarely! It is important to have a common view, not only to eliminate arguments, but also because eating out is expensive.

- What is your view of **giving**? Remember that God owns it all and He loves a hilarious giver! (2 Corinthians 9:7).

Your first source for answers to principles to guide you should be the Bible. Additionally, I encourage you to get Christian pre-marital counselling that includes money management.

As you begin the marriage, save 100% of the wife's income if you plan to start a family. Why the wife's income? Her income is the one that will be stopped if she takes time off to raise children. If you agree that dad will be a stay-at-home dad to raise the kids, save 100% of his income instead. The bottom line is this: Start to learn to live on one salary early if you plan for either husband or wife to stay home and raise the kids.

Even if you have been married for several years and one spouse will not stay at home, try to use one income only in the family budget while saving the other. It is never too late to try to live on one income and save the other. Certainly it will be more difficult the longer you are married, but not impossible. Of course, I am suggesting that both incomes be pooled, though allocated in this manner. I have seen couples who manage money as singles—each spending as he decides! This means neither partner has the full picture when making decisions. This approach encourages the "my-money-your-money" syndrome, which ignores that it's God's money! Allocate the income to be saved to the **Capital Fund**.

To operate the **PEACE** system, one person should record spending,[2] but both should develop the **Plan and**

Estimate (the budget). Both should agree on an **upper limit** of spending, beyond which the **Affordability Index** applies. Both should participate in the **control phase** of the **PEACE** system (ACT, Compare, and Execute), particularly the **executing** of changes to stay on course to achieve the **goals**.

Children

The money management principles for children and adults are identical. Proverbs 22:6 states, "Train children in the right way, and when old, they will not stray." The key, therefore, is to let your children observe you controlling money. Be their example so their instinctive responses will be the "right way" they saw their mom and dad functioning.

Teach your children to depend on Christ. Let them observe you doing so. I got a wake-up call about 19 years ago when Keisha (my daughter, then 10 years old) designed a special card titled, "To: Father." Below this title on the front, she drew Confucius. It was an excellent drawing in great detail. He was dressed in a blue robe, arms crossed in front, and he wore a traditional Chinese hat.

Keisha, Shabbir (my son), and Doreen signed the card and presented it to me. It contained this quotation, which they claimed was from (...you guessed, Confucius!): **"The nobler man first practiceth what he preacheth and afterwards preacheth according to his practice."** Wow! What a powerful message! I got it then and I am continually aware of it today. Yes, this is exactly what our Lord teaches us. I must ensure that I walk my talk! This card is hung in my study where I see it daily. I thank God for the openness and love of my family that led to this wake-up call!

At around age six or seven, when they start to appreciate that **you need money** to buy things for them, give each of your children an allowance, no matter how small. Let them earn the allowance by doing a few small chores so they may develop a responsible attitude towards work. From this allowance, teach them to give—including a tithe, to save, and to budget. Yes, to budget using the **PEACE** system, but keep it simple!

Teach them to set realistic goals and to work diligently to achieve these goals. It has been a joy to watch Bill and Keisha start our seven-year-old granddaughter, Adrienne, with an allowance from which she is tithing and saving! Presently, she is not as happy with tithing as with saving!

Never give your young children loans! Teach them to save for their purchases. Give them the keys to unlock their potential! Let them see Christ in you.

As your children mature, the chores should change along with the allowance. For a few years before Shabbir left home for university in British Columbia, he and I had a formal, written, annual snow removal contract (Doreen was his self-appointed lawyer). This included my responsibilities and his. I provided a snow blower in good working condition and he had to ensure that our driveway was cleared completely before seven a.m. whenever it snowed. I paid him the going market rate and he had to perform. The contract included a penalty clause for non-performance to an agreed standard, and an incentive clause for performance beyond that standard. I am happy to report that I was never delayed because of his poor performance. Indeed, most years he earned a bonus.

Encourage your **teenage children** to develop goals and plans, and to allocate budgets for the following expense elements:

- **Giving**: They should develop an instinctive response to give at least 10% of all income received.
- **Saving**: Encourage them to save for specific purchases.
- **Capital Fund**: This is the basis for them to enter adulthood debt-free and to continue in that manner. **They should save 50% of all income.** Unlike the savings account from which they may withdraw to purchase specific items, they should not use their **Capital Fund** except for large capital items such as: a car, wedding expenses, university education expenses, down payment on a home, purchase and repairs of appliances, etc. Their **Capital Fund** is for the same purposes as yours, except they will start it early!
- **Clothing**: They should buy all their clothes from this budget.
- **Entertainment**: This item is essential. The main purpose is for them to value the cost of eating out, going to the movies, video rentals, etc. Eating out can become expensive even at fast food restaurants!

Both Keisha and Shabbir managed budgets while at university/Bible college in their teens. Each studied in a different province from where we were living at the time. We developed budgets with them jointly and held them responsible to achieve them. Monthly, each sent us actual expenses compared with budgets, plus receipts for expenses, to receive reimbursement for amounts spent.

Finally, hold your children accountable for work "contracted" and achievement of goals. Teach them to develop spending habits that honour God. Let them make decisions where feasible, and make mistakes in the process. Teach them to learn from these mistakes. This is tough. Nevertheless, allow them this freedom, but be prepared to rescue them from harm. Praise and encourage them along the way. Most importantly, let them know that you love them unconditionally, as Jesus loves each of us.

Think About This

How committed are you to follow Christ? Like the pig for your bacon or the chicken for your egg?

Chapter Notes:

[1] 1 Corinthians 7:12-14

[2] Refer to Chapter 7 for discussion on recording your spending on the *PEACE* Budget Worksheet (PBW).

Section III

Selected Spending Decisions

*The More Time Spent in His Word,
the Clearer His "Voice,"
and the More Automatic
Your Dependence on Him*

10

Insurance

Insurance is a means to guarantee against a future loss. It entails payment of an amount **(the "premium")** to a company **(the "insurer")** who will pay a predetermined sum of money **(the "insured amount")** to a specific person **(the "beneficiary")** if a specific risk develops. Joshua is contemplating paying a premium of $250 per year to an insurer, Redemption Insurance Company, who will undertake to pay $250,000 to his beneficiary, Rebecca, his wife, when he dies.

You must answer the following questions before buying insurance:

- What is the risk to be covered?
- How much insurance do I need?

Let's look at five types of insurance:

- Life
- Mortgage
- Homeowner's
- Disability
- Equipment and Appliances (otherwise referred to as Extended Warranties)

Why Life Insurance?

The purpose of life insurance is to ensure that the **beneficiary** receives enough income from the insurance policy to replace the regular income and to pay funeral and other related expenses of the person who died **(the "insured")**. The risk to be covered is the loss of income on the death of the **insured**. To assess income loss, we need to consider not only present income but also future income.

Assume that Table I in Chapter 3 and Appendix I show Joshua and Rebecca's net worth and salaries respectively. How much insurance would they need so they would be no worse off on the death of either one? Rebecca would require an amount that, on Joshua's death, would replace his annual income of $37,800, plus a one-time expense for funeral and related expenses of, say, $6000. This excludes inflation and future salary increases.

If Joshua and Rebecca decided that $50,000 per year would be a more appropriate income for Rebecca on his death, the calculation of insurance coverage would be based on this amount. They would decide on the type of life insurance Joshua needed and would get a quotation for the cost of this insurance from different sources, including the Internet. The premium to replace income of $50,000 per year, plus funeral expenses of $6000, would be based on several inputs: **interest rate (say 7%), age, smoking habit, specific life expectancy, and so on**. Each situation is different.

Who Should Take Out Life Insurance

The person (in our example, Joshua) whose income-loss on death will be missed by those (Rebecca) who rely on his income (we refer to these persons as "**dependents**"). Sometimes insurance agents will sell newly-weds insurance on the life of both husband and wife. In our example, **Rebecca, who has no income,** should not spend money on life insurance premiums. Joshua should ensure that he would have enough money to pay Rebecca's funeral expenses if she died. He would not take out insurance for loss of her income.

As your net worth and income increases, review your situation, because your insurance needs may diminish since your dependents may have enough income from your investments!

Who Should Not Take Out Life Insurance

Anyone who has no dependents and who has enough savings to pay all expenses on death. There are exceptions. Individuals may wish to have life insurance so their favourite charities may receive the insured amounts when they die.

Different Types of Life Insurance

What type of life insurance should you have? There are two broad classes of life insurance: (a) **Term,** and (b) **Whole Life, Universal Life, or others that build cash reserves.**

Term life insurance is basic. It exists for a fixed period and the insured must renew it afterwards. It represents payment of a premium for coverage of a fixed amount for a specific period. For example, Joshua may pay $250 per year for insurance coverage of $250,000 for ten years. After ten years, Joshua would have no insurance.

If Joshua died within 10 years, the Redemption Insurance Company would pay Rebecca $250,000. If he lived beyond the tenth year, he would have to renew his insurance coverage. By then, it would be more expensive, say, over $400 per year for the same $250,000 coverage. The older you are, the more expensive the coverage. However, the older you are, the more savings/investments you are likely to have accumulated and the lower your insurance needs!

Whole life or Universal life insurance **or other cash reserves type policies** include a "cash build-up" or savings feature in addition to the term life insurance coverage, and do not need to be renewed periodically. For the same coverage of $250,000, Joshua would pay, say, $350 per year of which, say, $100 would represent excess premium over term insurance. Simplistically, the company would invest this excess and retain a portion of the investment income as profit and allocate the balance to the insured account. This is how "cash builds up" and becomes available for the individual to borrow, and ultimately, could reduce the need for the person to pay premiums.

You would be allowed to borrow against the accumulated savings at an interest rate lower than what you might pay at a bank, but higher than what your regular savings would earn. However, if you are a good steward of God's resources, why would you allow an insurance company to accumulate your savings to lend to you at a rate higher than your savings are earning? Normally, it does not make sense to do this. You would be much better off using the increased premium (that is, the difference in premium between **whole life and term**) to invest in a mutual fund.[1] This way the insurance company does not benefit from your savings!

Each situation is special, however, and I urge you to consult an independent financial adviser before buying life insurance. Do not be guided by an insurance salesman to prescribe your insurance needs. Ensure that you understand all options, including term, whole life, and mixtures of each. If you choose whole life or other similar policies that accumulate cash reserves, understand the reason! Generally, the insurance company will reap some benefits!

Mortgage Insurance

If Joshua borrowed $50,000 from a bank to buy a house, the bank would get its name on the title of the property. If Joshua sold the property, the new buyer would have known beforehand that the bank was a "co-owner" up to the value of its loan. We call this loan a mortgage. If Joshua died before he paid off the loan, the bank would have two options. Sell the house and give Rebecca the difference between the amount they received on sale and the balance of the loan, or allow Rebecca to assume this loan and repay it.

To prevent either of these events, Joshua could insure his life when he got the loan from the bank for the full value of the mortgage loan. This would supplement his regular life insurance coverage that we discussed already.

The risk for mortgage life insurance is the same as for normal life insurance. However, Joshua would buy insurance for the value of the mortgage loan and not for his annual income.

Disability Insurance

Often we overlook this area. Life insurance protects against the loss of income at death. Disability insurance protects against the loss of income if you become disabled. Determine where the risk exists and how much insurance you need using the same principles as for life insurance.

Homeowner's Insurance

So far, we have looked at insuring against the risk of loss of income. There is another class of insurance that protects against the risk to property. It's called "Homeowner's Insurance." Homeowner policies protect against damage to the home, and include coverage of your personal belongings and of your personal liability. The latter is to protect the insured and his family against claims resulting from losses caused by accidents on the home premises.

Insure your home for the replacement cost, which is the estimated cost of rebuilding your home if it was damaged. Normally, the insurance policy will include coverage of your personal belongings at about 40-60% of the coverage of the home. However, prepare a listing of your personal property and value each at its replacement cost—this is the value at which to insure your personal belongings, even if it is more than 50% of the value of the house.

With the homeowner's insurance package is personal liability coverage for accidents in the home. Some homeowner's policies have built-in coverage of $100,000 to $300,000, which may be adequate. For a small increment in premium, you can increase this coverage to one million dollars. Review your situation with an independent financial adviser and decide how much coverage you need.

Equipment and Appliances Insurance

What is the risk relative to your equipment and appliances? That you will start to have problems with your appliances immediately after the regular warranty period expires. When you buy a TV, VCR, refrigerator, stove, etc., the salesperson will ask you quite casually to spend an extra $50 or $100 to buy this insurance. Paying this amount would extend your warranty coverage!

We have never taken this coverage and we have never regretted those decisions. Generally, **I do not think this expense is necessary**. These appliances will last for many years before you need to repair them. Typically, if there are problems, they will arise in the early period when the equipment is under warranty. It is unusual for them to require repairs during the early years. Beware! This expense is merely a source of extra profit for the company selling the product. Never buy extended warranty without careful consideration. Preventing the need for this expenditure was one reason I developed the **Capital Fund**. You should be putting aside a small amount each month to cover future repairs and replacement of equipment and appliances. Then you will not need these extended warranties!

Finally, before buying insurance, consult an independent financial adviser and explain your situation. Do not rely on the advice of an insurance agent. This person may have good intentions, but she will benefit from selling you insurance. Therefore, her advice may not be objective.

Think About This

Truly, how much insurance do I need?
Jesus Christ!
What is the risk to be covered? Being lost!

Chapter Notes:

[1] A Mutual Fund is an organization that invests pooled funds of many depositors. Usually a professional manager manages it. Mutual Funds tend to specialize, each with a different investment objective. Examples of different funds are as follows: money market (typically government bonds), income, "balanced," Latin America, US growth and so on.

11

Purchasing Versus Renting a Home

What Purchasing Your Home Entails

In the 1960s through to the early 1980s, apart from a few brief periods, when you bought your home you would have established the base for the most predictable source of major, tax-free capital gains in your lifetime! Today, or subsequently, when you sell that home (prior to retirement or to upgrade to a larger home), you would expect to receive a tax-free gain substantially larger than the rate of inflation! Right? Yes, but that was for houses bought then! In some housing markets, the situation is different for houses purchased since the mid-1980s.

How times have changed! In the early 1980s, North

Americans went crazy! The greed about which we spoke in Chapter 2 was rampant! Among other things, housing prices soured! Canadian real estate markets, particularly in Vancouver and Toronto, sizzled until the mid-1980s when prices fell!

Today, many houses are selling at less than their 1989 values. No longer can you assume that housing prices will appreciate at a rate significantly greater than inflation, or even at the rate of inflation! Table VII shows selected housing prices in the Toronto and Montreal areas for 1998 and 1989; the 1998 prices are between 5 and 15% lower than the 1989 prices.

Does this mean that you should not own your home? Of course not! It means merely that you should know why you want to buy rather than rent a home—do not buy primarily to get a capital gain! Your home is not—should never have been—an investment in which you speculate. Use the same processes and spending aids to buy a home as you apply to all major spending decisions—**GAS, PEACE, PLANE, and Affordability Index.**

In recent years, as mortgage rates (indeed interest rates generally) fell, many people bought the houses/apartments that they were renting because monthly mortgage payments on those houses were less than their monthly rentals. Several of these folks did not appreciate fully that owning a home entailed more than a mortgage payment. Consequently, they had difficulty meeting all their housing expenses after buying their home.

Table VII: Housing Prices[1] (Detached Bungalow) in Selected Areas

1998 & 1989 ($000)

Detached Bungalow	1998(A)	1989(B)	(A) as % of (B)
Toronto Area			
Markham	232	285	81%
Oakville	200	210	95%
Scarborough-Agincourt	213	250	85%
Montreal Area			
Beaconsfield	118	130	91%
Dorval	104	114	91%
Brossard	105	110	95%

Owning a home requires the following annual (except otherwise noted) expenses:

- Mortgage payment which **may increase or decrease** over time (I recall 12-15% mortgage interest rates in the mid '80s compared with 7-8% now!);
- Property insurance;
- Repairs and maintenance;
- Property taxes/school taxes;
- Upkeep of property;
- Heat and lighting payments.
- Transfer taxes in some provinces—paid once at purchase;
- Other expenses including one-off legal fees and several small charges related to your mortgage and property title.

Normally, when you own your home, you build equity in the house as you reduce your mortgage, but you become exposed to a loss of property value if the housing market falls. However, this exposure should not be an issue because you would not buy your principal residence with a resale plan in mind!

What Renting Entails

Renting a house, on the other hand, includes a monthly payment with responsibility to upkeep the grounds and sometimes responsibility for heating and lighting. You have no further expenses. However, you do not build equity in the house from your monthly rent; neither are you open to the risk of loss of property value.

Depending on your mortgage term (see Composition of a Mortgage Payment below for explanation), mortgage rates (thus your mortgage payment) may vary significantly over time; whereas for many properties, monthly rental rates will tend to change in a much narrower range.

Issues to Consider to Evaluate the Rent Versus Buy Decision

Before evaluating the rent/buy decision, review the **three critical money management steps discussed in Chapter 3**. Afterwards, integrate your **Life Goals** and your **budget goals** with your aspirations to own your home. These goals must be compatible with each other!

Intuitively, it may seem that owning must be better than renting! Sure, you build equity when you own, but you may not be able to assume the cost of owning along with needed expenses to achieve other **Life Goals!**

Thus, with your **Life Goals** and the **GAS** principle as focal points, evaluate the rent versus buy options only after considering carefully the following matters:

- **The state of your net worth generally and your Financial Health Goals** specifically: In Chapter 3, I mentioned the 30% (of gross income) rule of thumb for mortgage payments, property taxes, and utility bills. I mentioned then also that this was but one parameter to consider because the key indicators were your financial health goals.

- Your **Capital Fund** balance: Do you have enough for the down payment and other commitments? If you do not have the down payment saved in your **Capital Fund**, you cannot afford to buy the house!

- Your preliminary **budgets for housing expenses**, both to rent and to buy: Will you be able to accommodate, in your existing household budget, additional expenses resulting from buying? What sacrifices must you make to do so? How realistic is this?

- Your **family situation**: How much space will you need? Are you and your wife planning to have a child shortly?

- Current and projected **economic conditions**: What is the state of the economy generally and the housing market particularly? Booming? Flat?

- **Financial benefits** available for first time home-buyers. Some provinces offer incentives to first time homebuyers. Additionally, first time buyers may use up to $20,000 from their RRSP account tax free, as a loan to themselves for the down payment on their homes.[2]

- Your **job circumstance**: Are you likely to remain at your current employer in the short-term? Are you likely to be transferred to a different location? What is the company's policy if you are required to move and you sell your home at a loss? In almost thirty years, we moved nine times and these were questions we answered each time.

Buying a house will likely be the single most expensive expenditure you will incur in your lifetime. Perform the above analyses systematically, but do not procrastinate. Ultimately, you must face decisions that you put off today! Why not tackle them now? The bottom line is this: Your expenses for renting and for owning a home will differ.

Several sources exist to help you perform the rent versus buy number crunching analyses, including the Internet. Some books and financial advisers will tell you to perform a net present value ("NPV")[3] computation for which you need an estimate of annual costs of renting and of owning. Further, you need, among other things, the **highly subjective,** estimated future selling price of the house! Nobody will know this number and probably it will influence the results of the computation!

Do not rely on this NPV analysis. Your principal residence is not an investment property! Do not buy your home with a view to reselling it in the short-term. If you believe you may have to sell the property shortly after purchase, rent instead of buy. If you are uncomfortable with high housing prices, wait until prices fall.

Establish your price range based on your purchasing criteria and your budget, and buy when your preferred conditions exist. Otherwise rent.

This rent/buy decision is important and will affect your budget. Do not take it in isolation. Follow the **GAS** principle rigorously, particularly **Key Truth #3: Seek First His Kingdom and Submit Your Requests to Him**!

Buying the Home

If you decided to buy a home, Appendix IV shows a form that my wife and I used successfully to assist us in buying houses over the years during our nine job-related transfers. Typically, we would buy a house within three days of visiting a location because we prepared extensively ahead of our visit. Of course, if you are moving within the same area, the process will be much simpler; visiting the location will not be an issue. Our moves were usually outside of Quebec (our home province) or outside of Canada.

Below are some of the inputs into the decision on the location. We tried to resolve most of the issues before visiting the new location to house shop. With the Internet and other means available today, it is much easier to do preparatory screening to reduce physical presence at the location. The result of these decisions will affect your household budget:

- **Amenities** required in the new area.

- **Transportation** requirements. This will determine the method of commuting to work, commuting time needed, and cost of commuting. When we moved to Tokyo, Japan, we decided that I would commute by train, thus we needed to live close to necessary facilities.

- **Recreational** facilities (for each season).
- **Security**.
- Available **schools.**
- Property tax rates.
- Proximity to a library.
- Proximity to shopping, medical facilities, etc.
- Proximity to parks—very helpful with young kids.

Each of the above will have a different level of importance to your decision. Identify and rank the top three and include as part of your goals. Before you go shopping for a house, prepare a budget with a definite upper limit. Agree with your spouse on key goals and criteria for the house you wish to buy, such as size, number of bedrooms, finished/unfinished basement, type of kitchen, and so on.

Arrange your mortgage; confirm the availability of the down payment; and select a real estate agent ("agent"). Interview him. Ask about his experience and ask him to give you the names of two persons whom he helped to **buy** (not sell) their house. Check these references carefully.

The seller pays the agent, who deducts his commission from the selling price. Indeed, both agents—yours and the seller's—receive their commissions from the selling price. Therefore, do not expect your agent to look after your interests exclusively. Nevertheless, though not paid by you for this transaction, your agent works for you. Unless you have some basis to trust your agent, do not disclose to him your **final price.** Tell him a listing price[4] range and the other criteria (such as proximity to a train station) that you have decided on from which he may select houses for you to visit.

Learn the sale process in detail. Ask as many questions as necessary until you understand fully all the nuances! Prepare, prepare, and prepare! Nothing beats preparation. When you visit the location, request the agent to schedule several appointments in sequence.

During your house shopping trip, don't become overtly attached to one house only! Otherwise, you will end up buying it at what I call an "emotional" price. Use Appendix IV as you visit each house. You and your spouse should make separate notes on each house. At the end of each day, compare notes and prepare a list of the top three houses you have seen thus far. Prioritize them based on previously agreed-upon criteria. Repeat the process daily, changing the top three as necessary. When you decide to stop visiting houses, revisit each of the top three for a more thorough inspection to clarify issues you noted during the previous visit.

Afterwards, make an offer[5] on your number one choice, knowing that you are happy with your two other selections; therefore, you could walk away from this house if the price isn't right! Naturally, you will do your best to get your number one choice, but you will not exceed your original maximum price. If you and your spouse believe that you must increase your maximum price, repeat the process above to set the new limit.

After selecting one house, but before you finalize the purchase, get an independent, professional building inspector to give you a report on the property. It would not be unusual for him to identify $10,000 of urgent repairs that you did not notice! This becomes part of the final price negotiations.

The 1996 Canada Census[6] reported the statistics in Table VIII for privately rented and privately owned dwellings. Of the 64% who owned occupied dwellings in Canada in 1996, about half (or 32%) had no mortgage. In 1987, 62% owned rather than rented in Canada, and about half also had no mortgage.[7]

Table VIII: Number of Rented and Owned Private Dwellings

Location	# Owned (A)	# Rented (B)	(A) % of Total (A+B)
Canada	6,877,780	3,905,145	64%
Ontario	2,523,385	1,396,145	64%
Quebec	1,593,600	1,225,305	57%
Montreal	649,895	691,375	48%

Composition of a Mortgage Payment

As we saw earlier, your mortgage is the loan the bank or other institution will advance to you using your house as security. If you cannot repay this loan, the institution will sell your house and, from the proceeds of sale, deduct the amount owing to them. They will give you any excess above their loan balance.

How does the financial institution compute your mortgage payment? Table IX shows a simplistic analysis of annual mortgage payments, highlighting the principal and interest components.

Observe how the interest component reduces and the principal component increases with each payment.

Thus, a one-off principal payment, in addition to the regular mortgage payment, ensures a more rapid reduction of the principal. View your mortgage payment as your monthly rental plus an increasing savings component![8]

Table IX: Simplistic Mortgage Amortization Schedule (Assuming Annual Payment)

Year	Start Balance	Payment	10% Interest	Principal Part
1	1000	263.80	100.00	163.80
2	836.2	263.80	83.62	180.18
3	656.0	263.80	65.60	198.20
4	457.8	263.80	45.78	218.02
5	239.8	263.80	23.98	239.82

Normally, your mortgage is more complex. In my example in Table IX, I assumed that the mortgage term and the amortization period were the same; typically, they are not. The mortgage term represents the life of the agreement with the financial institution—six months, one year, five years, and so on. Your monthly payment will be the same during the term, at the end of which you may re-negotiate the mortgage. Ask your financial institution about available mortgage terms. Understand the differences between open and closed, and fixed and variable rate mortgages.[9]

How do you decide what term to select? Be guided primarily by your budget and the general direction of interest rates and inflation rate. In the early 1980s, when interest rates and inflation were high and rising, it was prudent to arrange a term with a fixed rate for about one year so that you knew your cost at least one year ahead. You would not set the term for ten years! Today, with interest rates and the inflation rate low, you may choose to fix your term (and rate) for five, ten, or more years.

Of course, you may choose an interim position, say, of an open mortgage of six months, if you believed interest rates were trending down. After six months, you would fix the rate for five, ten, or more years. This is not a science. Beware! Ensure that you understand your options and seek guidance if necessary.

Irrespective of the mortgage term, you must decide over what period you wish to repay the entire mortgage; this is the amortization period—20, 25, 30 years. The longer the amortization period, the longer to repay the principal. Table X shows examples of amortization periods of 20 and 25 years, and monthly and bi-weekly (26 per year) payments. Notice the difference in interest paid over the life of the mortgages!

Since mortgage interest on your principal residence is not a deductible expense for tax purposes in Canada, if your marginal tax rate is 40%, you must earn $100[10] to pay $60 of mortgage. This concept was discussed in Chapter 4.

Table X: Repayment of $100,000 Mortgage With Different Assumptions

	Monthly Payment	Bi-Weekly Payment	Monthly Payment	Bi-Weekly Payment
Mort. Amt	$100,000	$100,000	$100,000	$100,000
Int. Rate	10 %	10%	10%	10%
Mort. Term	5 years	5 years	5 years	5 years
Amortization	20 years	20 years	25 years	25 years
Payment	$952	$438	$894	$412
Int. Paid over Life of Loan	$128,402	$127,898	$168,343	$167,751
Bal. at End of Term	$89,588	$89,587	$93,992	$93,991
Princ. Paid at End of Term	$10,412	$10,413	$6,008	$6,009

Selling the Home

Selling your home requires as much preparation as buying does. First, you identify your goals. Next, you apply rigorously the **Planning and Estimating** aspects of the **PEACE** system. Then, you select an agent to whom you outline your objectives. The reason you are selling will be critical to the **Acting** or implementing stage. The more time-flexibility available, the longer you can wait for your target price.

Research the market with the agent and set a realistic final price. Remember, time is money (refer back to Chapter 3)! It may be better to accept a lower price sooner, rather than a higher price much later!

Mortgage Refinancing

Sometimes falling interest rates will prompt some individuals to consider renegotiating their mortgages. In other words, to save money, **it would appear** that you should repay your existing mortgage and get a new one at a lower interest rate. Before I review an example, I should remind you that when your mortgage term expires, you will be able to renegotiate your mortgage, penalty free. Thus, your first action should be to determine the length of the unexpired term of your mortgage.

If you bought your home at what you thought was a great interest rate, and interest rates fell, how would you approach a refinancing or renegotiating of your mortgage rate? Here are the principles:

- Look at the total picture using a net present value ("NPV") analysis. Do not look exclusively at the original mortgage payment at the high rate and the revised payment at the new rate.

- The bank or financial institution ("institution") will not be out of pocket by refinancing/renegotiating ("renegotiating"). Why would they allow you to break a contract so they become worse off and you become better off? They won't! They will recover the NPV of the interest rate differential (that is, the difference between the existing rate of 9% and the new rate of 7%) for the unexpired mortgage term. Thus, when you renegotiate at 7%, the institution will compute the NPV of the amount of interest they will lose (2%) and charge this to you as a penalty, so they are no worse off.

- You can benefit from renegotiating your mortgage as follows:
  a) You renegotiate an extended mortgage term (say from five to seven years), and
  b) Interest rates increase during the extension (say from 7% to 10%), and
  c) The NPV of this interest rate increase during the extension exceeds the NPV of the penalty paid.
  d) Note, however, that you will never know beforehand if interest rates will increase during the extension!

Each case is different and will be influenced significantly by two factors: the percentage reduction in the mortgage interest rate, and the length of the unexpired mortgage term. Depending on these two factors, the institution may propose a blended[11] rate to cushion the impact of its penalty.

Before you renegotiate, perform the computation below:

Assume you bought your home several years ago, and currently, your mortgage outstanding is $90,000 at an interest rate of **9%**. Presently, the unexpired term is five years, and the mortgage is being amortized over twenty years. Today, mortgage rates have fallen to **7%**. Should you refinance? **These are the facts based on semi-annual compounding**:

- **Your current annual** mortgage payment at **9%** is **$9600** (one-twelfth paid monthly).
- **The annual** payment at **7%** (excluding refinancing penalties) would be **$8304** (one-twelfth paid monthly).

- **Annual savings** (excluding penalties) will be **$1296 ($9600-$8304) over five years**.

- Rough estimate of the institution's penalty charge is **$7000** (representing the NPV of the interest rate differential of 2% over five years—the unexpired term).

Your decision should be based solely on the lower of these two amounts: the NPV of your projected annual savings of $1296 over the unexpired mortgage term, versus the NPV of the institution's penalty charge. The NPV at 7% of the annual savings of $1296 (computed monthly), over five years, is about $5,500. Therefore, if you had to pay the penalty of $7000 either up-front or over the unexpired term only, it would be more expensive to refinance.

The institution may offer a blended rate to **spread the $7000 over the new mortgage term of, say, seven years.** Thus, it may add, say, $110 per month to the proposed monthly payment referred to above[12] to recover $7000 over seven years (if this was the new term). Nevertheless, the bottom line is this: The institution will not lose but will recover its penalty either as a lump sum or over the new mortgage term. As I said earlier, generally, it does not pay to refinance your mortgage except for the following situation:

- You extend the mortgage term (say, from five to seven years), and

- The mortgage interest rate increases during the extension (say, from 7% to 10%), and

- The NPV of increases in the mortgage interest

rate during the extended period exceeds the NPV of the penalty to be paid.

If the institution is no worse off, you are likely to be no better off! See an independent financial adviser to guide you through this process.

Think About This

Being sensitive and responsive to God's will means denying self and sometimes doing what is unnatural.

Chapter Notes:

[1] Royal LePage, Survey of Canadian House Prices, Historical Data—Quebec—July 1989; Quebec—Jan 1998; Ontario—July 1989; Ontario 1998.

[2] See Chapter 13 where I discuss RRSPs. Generally, I discourage this practice of borrowing from your RRSP. Start a Capital Fund and use amounts from this source as your down payment.

[3] Net Present Value: The present value (today's value) of future cash flows, discounted (the process of finding today's value of a series of future cash flows) at a specific interest rate (your average cost of borrowing), minus an initial outlay, where relevant.

[4] This is the advertised price. Typically, you will buy the house for less. Research the current pattern in the area. What percentage of listing prices have been final selling prices? This is an important input to help you decide your final price.

[5] This is a formal process where you stipulate the price and conditions under which you are prepared to buy the house. Understand it before you start house shopping.

6 1996 Census Statistical Profile, Family and Dwelling Statistics.

7 Statistics Canada, Households by Dwelling Characteristics, Catalogue no. 64-202-RPB.

8 Table IX shows the split of your mortgage payment between interest and principal. The savings component in each payment is the amount allocated to principal. Of course, if housing prices fall below your cost, the "savings" may be offset.

9 With an **open** mortgage, you can repay the principal anytime without a penalty. For a **closed** mortgage, you pay a penalty if you repay before the term expires. There are also **Variable Rate Mortgages** and **Fixed Rate Mortgages**. A **Variable Rate Mortgage** is a mortgage with fixed payments, but which allows for fluctuation in interest rates due to changing market conditions. Changes in the interest rate will determine how much of each payment will go toward the principal. Thus, if the mortgage interest rate increases, the allocation to principal as in Table IX will decrease and vice versa. A **Fixed Rate Mortgage** is a mortgage with fixed payments and the interest rate does not change during the mortgage term. Table IX shows the impact of a fixed rate mortgage.

10 Income of $100 at a 40% tax rate is equal to taxes of $40 and a disposable income of $60.

11 Blending merely apportions the penalty over the new term (over seven years in our example) so that your monthly payment will be lower than the current level. Still, you pay the penalty.

12 This extra payment will result in a blended rate greater than 7%.

12

Leasing Versus Buying a Car

To understand fully the implications of leasing a car, I will comment briefly on leasing generally. Prior to the 1950s, leasing was associated with real estate (land and buildings). Today, it is possible to lease almost every asset, primarily because leasing has become an established form of borrowing. Let's look briefly at three situations:

- Sale and leaseback
- Service leases
- Financial leases

Sale and Leaseback

Under this arrangement, a company needs cash and decides to sell an asset to a finance company. However, because it needs the asset also, it contracts to use the asset for a fee. Thus, it may sell the asset for $100,000 and immediately leases it back for, say, $12,000 per year. Here, the decision is driven by the need for cash. Nothing will vary when the transaction is completed apart from the change in ownership. The company will continue to operate and maintain the asset.

Service (or Operating) Leases

IBM pioneered this type of lease. The **lessor** (the company that owns the asset and offers the lease) owns the asset and provides it for use by the **lessee** (the person or company that will use the asset). Typically, the lessor is responsible to maintain the asset. In our office, we lease computers, office plants and other items. Following are a few unique features to this type of lease:

- The lease tends to be short-term and cancelable at any time.
- Lease payments do not cover the full cost of each asset.
- The lease period usually is less than the life of the asset.
- The same asset may be leased sequentially to others (the plants that I return today may be leased to you tomorrow).

Financial Leases

This is the category that applies to individuals. Generally, it is a convenient way for people to buy assets they cannot afford! These folks do not separate each asset acquisition decision into two necessary components. First, the need! Do I need it? Next, the affordability! How do I pay for it?

Decide if you need the asset by applying the **GAS** principle. Then employ the **PLANE** spending analysis and the **Affordability Index.** Borrow to buy a home or, under special situations, to buy a car only.

Today, you can lease almost any asset. However, the car is one of the most popular assets that individuals lease. As car prices soared, manufacturers devised a clever strategy to get people to drive cars they can't afford, and be happy! By focussing on a "modest" monthly payment, manufacturers have created the illusion that leasing a car is a great deal for you and me! Leasing adds a layer of complexity to purchasing a car that the general public does not fully understand; thus, they lease cars!

What does leasing a car entail? Typically, a person who decides to acquire a car selects it from the manufacturer **(Ford),** who arranges with its finance company to buy the car. The finance company **(the lessor)** then enters into an agreement **(a "lease")** with you or me, whereby we pay a fixed monthly amount **(the "lease payment")** for a specified period to operate and maintain the car. At the end of the period, you return the car to the lessor. Probably you will take a more expensive car for the second lease, and the cycle resumes!

This is a financial lease that requires the lessee to maintain the car, as if he owned it. Equally, he will benefit from repairs covered by warranty like any owner. Further, there is a high but loose standard of maintenance that he must sustain throughout the lease period so that he returns the car to the lessor in "good" condition. Other features of this type of lease are as follows:

- The lessee cannot terminate the lease. It is for a fixed term.
- The manufacturer receives payment equal to the full price of the car, including a profit, from the lessor.
- The finance company, the lessor, will reflect its full cost plus a profit in the lease charged.

As I said before, generally leasing (without purchasing the car at the end of the lease) is more expensive than outright purchase because, among other things, at the end of the lease you return the car and restart the process! Table XI shows an example of an actual situation in Montreal in October 1999; the numbers include relevant taxes.

There are several important numbers in Table XI. You get the figures in the shaded area "A" to "H" from the lessor. The key numbers that will impact your decisions are shown in the final three rows, "M" to "O." Row "M" shows the NPV ($17,568) to lease then buy at the end of the lease term (4 years); this is the least expensive option. It is about $1100 less than the second option of outright purchase in the "Buy" column.

If you returned the car at the end of the lease and took another lease under the same terms, the NPV of $21,540 in row "N" is the highest of the three options. Consequently, if you planned to use the car beyond the expiration of the first lease, you would be better off to lease with the intention of buying the car at the end of the lease. Refer to Chapter 8 where I discussed the **Affordability Index** and the purchase of a car.

Finally, before you decide to lease a car, understand the process and the options, and seek help from an

Table XI: Analysis of Leasing Versus Buying a Car

	Input From the Lessor	Lease	Buy
A	Purchase price including taxes	$18,700	$21,527
B	Residual value to purchase at the end of 4 years	$7025	0
C	Financing—Interest rate	2.0%	2.8%
D	Lease Period/Loan Period—mos.	48	60
E	Kilometres allowed each year	20k	No limit
F	Down payment	0	0
G	Refundable deposit	$325	0
H	Monthly rate	$305	$385
	Payment Computations		
I	Annual payments (Hx12)	$3660	$4620
J	Payments for 4 years excl. residual (Ix4)	$14,640	$18,480
K	Total payments[1] incl. Residual (B+J)	$21,665	$18,480
L	Total payments for 5 yrs (K+I)		$23,100
	Net Present Value (NPV) Calculation[2]		
M	NPV of lease payments over 4 years plus NPV of residual payment in B to buy the car (NPV of individual components of items in row K)	$17,568[3]	
N	NPV of payments over 5 years under buy option (NPV of individual payments in L)		$18692
O	NPV if car turned in at year 4 and an identical new lease entered into for another 4 years	$21540	

independent financial adviser. Unless you plan to operate the vehicle for a limited period, you will be better off owning (including leasing then exercising the buy option) rather than leasing then returning the car to the lessor at the end of the lease period.

Think About This

Preparing a spending plan will not solve your problems but it will identify in advance your options to achieve your goals. You may then decide if and how you intend to live within your means!

Chapter Notes:

[1] This figure includes the "residual" because you decided to buy the car. Otherwise, the total lease payments would be $21665 - $7025 = $14640 as per row "J."

[2] I will remind you of the concept of Net Present Value: It is today's value of a series of expenses in the future discounted at a specific interest rate.

[3] This NPV excludes two potential expenses: Cost of mileage in excess of 20,000 kilometres per year, and expenses at the end of the lease that are necessary to return the car in an acceptable state of repair.

Section IV

Looking Beyond the Sunset

List the Many Blessings You Have Received
Then Tell Someone Today
of the Wonderful God We Serve

13

Registered Retirement Savings Plan (RRSP) and Registered Education Savings Plan (RESP)

Registered Retirement Savings Plan (RRSP) Contributions

The purpose of this chapter is to alert you to this truly great opportunity to save and earn a significant return on your savings! Each situation is unique, so consult a financial adviser to determine your actual RRSP entitlement. Understand the concepts so that you will be able to make informed decisions about your contribution.

As the name implies, an RRSP is a savings plan to which your annual contribution is tax deductible. Generally, the maximum annual allowable tax deduction is

18% of your earned income for the prior year (with an absolute ceiling, currently, of $13,500) less benefits accrued under your registered pension plans (RPPs) and deferred profit sharing plans (DPSPs) for the previous year. If you contribute less than your maximum allowable amount in one year, you may carry forward the shortfall to future years.

In Canada, you know it is February (apart from the cold weather!) because you are bombarded with requests to complete your RRSP contributions for the previous year; the deadline for contributions is the end of February.

Contribute your maximum each year. If you have not done this previously, plan to erase outstanding amounts quickly. I will illustrate the benefit of contributing to an RRSP in Table VII.

If you deposited your equivalent RRSP contribution of $6500 into any other account, you would not get a tax deduction. Neither would the income be sheltered. This is the reason to contribute your maximum. The benefit is great!

I have two caveats about RRSPs. First, **do not borrow** to maximize your contribution **unless you have the funds to repay the loan in full when you receive the partial tax refund.** In Table VII, your RRSP contribution was $6500 and your refund was $2925, which is $3575 short of the amount you would have had to borrow to contribute to your RRSP! I repeat, do not borrow to maximize your contribution unless you know how you will repay the full amount, in this case $6500.

My second warning concerns the Home Buyer's Plan. This 1992 modification allows a first-time home buyer

Table VII: RRSP Computation

	1997	1998	1999
Salary	$50,000		
Contribution to company pension plan (5%)	$2,500		
Marginal tax rate[1]	45%		
Maximum RRSP Contribution: (50,000 x 18%) = $9000 minus $2500	$6,500		
Tax Refund in April ($6500 x 45%)	**$2,925**		
Net cost to you ($6500 - $2925)	$3,575		
After one year—income (10% of $6500)		$650	
Tax saved (sheltered)— (45% of $650)		$293	
After two years—Total Investment	$7,150		
(Contribution plus interest— $6500 + $650)			
After two years—income (10% of $7150)			$715
Tax saved (45% of $715)			$322

From Table VII these are your benefits:

· Tax refund in April 1998 of $2,925 for tax year 1997.

· Tax sheltered in 1998 of $293[2]

· Tax sheltered in 1999 of $322

to borrow from his RRSP up to $20,000 tax free to purchase a home that must be used as his primary residence (not rental property). Naturally, there are restrictions, including repayment over a fixed consecutive period in equal annual amounts. If you miss or reduce an installment, you must pay tax on the amount of the shortfall. Thus, if you were to repay $2000 per year and you paid only $1500 in one year, you have to pay tax on ($2000 - $1500) $500.

What's my problem with the Home Buyer's Plan? Your RRSP is for your retirement. **Don't touch it**; let it grow! How's that for clarity! If you wish to buy a house, use your **Capital Fund** (you haven't forgotten about this, have you? Refer to Chapter 6) to save for the down payment.

In addition to your RRSP, your spouse should maximize her contribution based on the same principles. Whether or not your spouse has earned income, you can contribute on her behalf to an RRSP provided the total of your contribution and the amount you contribute to her RRSP does not exceed your maximum allowable deduction.

Where do you deposit your contribution? This is another positive feature of an RRSP. You have flexibility. You may deposit the funds in vehicles ranging from conservative types such as Guaranteed Investment Certificates (GICs), to aggressive vehicles such as equity funds that you "manage." Most persons go the safe GIC route. Although I do not recommend speculation, depending on your age, I would suggest that you invest in other safe investment instruments, such as certain balanced mutual funds. Discuss this aspect with your independent financial adviser.

Most people do not wish to get involved with managing their RRSP on a regular basis. I agree with them. This requires specific expertise and can be time-consuming. However, get to know the type of accounts that would be right for you and review them periodically. I have a self-directed RRSP account, which means I invest the funds directly. I can place the funds in Government Treasury Bills, leave them in cash, invest in the shares of a company listed on Canadian stock exchanges, or a combination. Further, I may invest up to 20% of the cost of my investment portfolio overseas.

I do not recommend a self-directed account for most individuals. However, although you may not have a self-directed account, you should be aware of how your account is being managed and where funds are invested.

Although in this book I will not discuss investing and investment strategies, remember the following when you consider investing your RRSP funds:

- The **GAS** principle.
- You are investing for the long-term; do not listen to those short-term-focussed Wall Street and Bay Street analysts who seem to use the stock market more for gambling than for prudent investing.
- Poor earnings by a company one or even two quarters do not necessarily indicate that a company will be doomed forever! The bottom line is do not speculate!
- You do not pay capital gains tax when you sell investments in your RRSP account.

What happens if you need funds urgently and your only source is your RRSP account? First, I challenge you to pray and seek to know God's will. Then, review the **PEACE**, the **PLANE**, and the **Affordability Index**. Next, re-examine your budget! Finally, go exploring in those areas about which we spoke in Chapter 6. If truly you must, then withdraw the funds, but you will pay taxes on the amount withdrawn.

In the year you turn age 69, you must choose one of the following:

- **Lump-sum withdrawal:** Cash received will be taxed in the year you receive it.

- **Convert your RRSP balance to an annuity:** This is a means to convert your lump sum into monthly payments for life or a fixed term. The monthly payments are taxed when received.

- **Convert to a Registered Retirement Income Fund (RRIF):** Probably this will be the best option. Essentially, this is like your RRSP except you must make withdrawals each year, excluding the year you set it up. You may keep the same investments that you had in your RRSP.

This decision is vital and you should consult your independent financial adviser.

Registered Education Savings Plan (RESP)

This is an excellent savings vehicle generally used by parents to save for their children's post-secondary education. It is an agreement between an individual and a person or organization whereby the individual makes contributions that accumulate tax-free in an account for the benefit of a beneficiary or beneficiaries. Generally there are no restrictions on who can be a beneficiary.

Over fifteen years ago I used this avenue to save for Keisha's education. Unlike an RRSP you do not get a tax deduction for the amounts you contribute to the RESP. When Keisha attended McGill University, she used the income from the RESP account to pay her fees. She declared that amount as income for tax purposes and paid no taxes because of her modest total income.

Since 1998, the Minister of Human Resources Development will pay a 20% **Canada Education Savings Grant (CESG)** on the first $2,000 of annual contributions made to all eligible RESPs of a qualifying beneficiary. The maximum CESG amount that a beneficiary can receive is $7,200. The grants, RESP contributions, and accumulated earnings will be part of the educational assistance payments paid out of the plan to the beneficiary. Payments to the beneficiary will be taxable. However, typically the beneficiary will have little or no income.

There is an annual limit of $4,000 and a lifetime limit of $42,000 on the amount that can be contributed to an RESP. These limits apply to each beneficiary regardless of the number of plans for a beneficiary (thus if Michel has a plan for Adrienne and Bill has a plan for Adrienne, the limits apply to the combined plans). Payments made to an RESP under the CESG program are not considered to be contributions to the plan.

Visit Canada Customs and Revenue Agency's website for more details of RESPs.

Think About This

Count your blessings.
Would you be prepared to give up any
for more money?

Chapter Notes:

[1] **Marginal Tax Rate:** The tax rate that applies to the last dollar of income that you earn.

[2] Income earned within the RRSP account is not taxed until you withdraw it. Thus, while it is being accumulated, it is "sheltered" from taxes. Notice that compound interest is at work here!

14

Estate Planning

What is Estate Planning?

Estate planning is the process of arranging to dispose of your assets when you die. It includes preparing a net worth statement and a will.[1] Before I accepted Christ as my Lord and my Saviour, I had great difficulty discussing this subject. Truly, I refused to think about it.

In retrospect, I realize why I would not talk about death. The thought of dying and not knowing what happened thereafter bothered me. Not anymore! Now I know that I have eternal life. I am sure that one day I will see Jesus face to face. Thus, I know death is nothing to fear; it is an inevitable occurrence for which we should plan.

Why Should We Prepare Wills?

Since we cannot take our possessions with us when we die, we should never become attached to them. We should hold them loosely. Meanwhile, we should pray and seek God's direction concerning their disposal when we die. If we don't leave instructions, governments will apply their rules! I am sure you would not want this! Lack of a will, quite likely, may cause anxiety for our remaining loved ones.

Who Should Prepare a Will and What Should It Contain?

Accordingly, everyone over 18 years of age should prepare a will, which should include some of the following:

- Distribution of assets, net of liabilities: Listing of specific assets[2] with names of persons and/or organizations to receive them, plus names of recipients of the balance of the estate—these recipients are called beneficiaries. Include also the names of alternative beneficiaries (including beneficiaries under a catastrophic situation where the family dies together) in case any die before you or chosen organizations cease to exist at your death.

- If you have minor children, name a guardian to care for them.

- Name of someone and an alternate (the "executor") to implement the instructions in your will, such as:
  - Paying funeral and related expenses;
  - Collecting money owing at death;

- Paying bills outstanding at death;
- Distributing your assets, after paying bills, to your beneficiaries;
- Other details, such as funeral arrangements.

My first will in my late 20s was simple. I left everything to my wife,[3] who reciprocated. Still, a lawyer prepared both! Although you can prepare your own will, I recommend strongly that you get professional help—even if your financial affairs are simple.

Sometimes you do not want to distribute all assets at death, so you establish a trust[4] within your will. Each trust has a beneficiary, or beneficiaries, who will receive income from assets in the trust. The beneficiary may receive portions of the capital (this is the value of what you owned less what you owed at death) at fixed periods, or at a later date when the trust is dissolved.

Currently, both my will and my wife's include trusts to receive a portion of our assets upon death. Here are three reasons to create a trust:

- You have young kids and would like to leave them a stream of annual income. The trustee would manage the assets and pay income to the children periodically.
- You wish to distribute income regularly or sporadically to charities.
- You wish to make periodic distribution of capital; you may require the total assets to be paid over a fixed period.

Review your wills occasionally and change them as necessary.

How to Prepare a Will

The key document you need to prepare your will is your net worth statement, with the supporting details of individual assets and liabilities. This shows details of what you own and what you owe. I repeat my recommendation that you seek professional advice to prepare a will.

Decide whether you need to see an independent financial adviser before you meet a lawyer. The former would prepare or assist you to prepare a net worth statement and would advise you on taxation and other financial aspects. It is important that you understand precisely your financial affairs before thinking about the complexities of the will. The lawyer would advise on the actual preparation of the will. You know your situation and you must make this call.

When you prepare your will, think of two goals: one for "before" and the other for "after," as follows:

- **Before** you die, leave clear instructions to your executor or executors to distribute your assets.

- Follow all legal procedures to prepare your will to ensure that **after** you die, your executor will settle the estate quickly and smoothly, according to your instructions.

You control the first objective. For the second, discuss with your lawyer the legal nuances that apply in your province and which you should follow. A Notary[5] prepared our wills in Quebec. We registered them for quick processing when necessary. If we did not notarize them, they could require more processing time at death.

Selecting an Executor

Who should be your executor? Should you use a professional firm? I mentioned the role of the executor already. Obviously, the person you choose should be capable of performing those duties. Additionally, she should have impeccable integrity, share your values, and be reliable. If you choose a professional, realize that the firm will charge a fee, probably a percent of your assets less your liabilities. Interview that firm and be comfortable with their capabilities to do the job as you require.

Keep your will in a safe place, such as with your lawyer. Tell your family and executor, if different, the location. Destroy all previous wills.

Power of Attorney

A power of attorney is a legal document in which one party gives another the right to act on his behalf. My wife and I give each other powers of attorney so each has the right to make decisions about the other. From our perspectives, it is necessary for two reasons.

- If one of us becomes incapable of functioning, the other can make necessary decisions.

- If one of us is out of town, the other can make urgent decisions that require consent of both of us.

We have found it almost indispensable because of my frequent overseas business trips. However, this is a personal matter that each couple must address as they see fit.

I would like to make this closing comment about the power of attorney. It should not change your regular decision-making processes! Use it for convenience and/or emergencies only! One person should not abuse it to make unilateral decisions! Apart from incapacity, it is a convenient method to implement joint decisions. The actions that I implement on my own using my wife's power of attorney to me all have her prior blessing, and vice versa.

Think About This

The Bible is the instruction manual for life. Live by it! Die by it!

Chapter Notes:

[1] A will is a document that shows, among other things, your desired distribution of your net assets when you die.

[2] Normally, you would not identify every asset you own in your will because you discard or replace some assets periodically. The professionals will tell you that if the estate will be divided, it is better to identify few specific assets and to allocate the balance of the estate in fixed proportions. That way there will be no problem if a specific asset was not separately identified.

[3] Although my wife is a stay-at-home-mom, she has a will because neither of us wants any government to decide on our asset distribution when we die.

[4] A Trust is property held by one party (the trustee) for the benefit of another (the beneficiary).

[5] A Notary is a member of the legal profession who specializes in non-litigious matters such as property issues and wills. A notarial will is prepared only in Quebec. Notarial wills settled in Quebec do not have to go through the verification and probate process when you die. In February 1999, a Notary charged $303 to prepare both my will and my wife's will.

15

Choosing a Financial Adviser

Would you attempt dental surgery on yourself? Would you try to remove your tonsils? Of course you wouldn't! So why would you try to manage your financial affairs without consulting a professional? Seek competent, expert advice to help you manage God's money using the tools we discussed earlier!

Many companies have extended their share option[1] plans to large groups of employees. They have savings plans, life insurance plans, and several benefit plans. You have direct access to savings bonds, RRSPs and RESPs. How do you take maximum advantage of available financial choices within the context of your Christian values? Generally, unless you are a trained financial professional, you will find your financial situation complex!

Often, in previous chapters, I encouraged you to consult an independent financial adviser to assist with aspects of this money management journey. I stressed the need for independence to avoid possible conflicts of interest.

Who Is a Financial Adviser?

Many persons call themselves financial advisers. Some sell mutual funds, life insurance, stocks and bonds, or other financial products. They may be knowledgeable, of the highest integrity, and have your interests at heart. Many would not knowingly give bad advice just to sell their products. Nevertheless, their recommendations may not be best suited to you. Therein lies the potential conflict of interest! An insurance agent's view of the quality of his company's products may differ from an independent financial adviser's!

Then, there are financial advisers who sell their services for a fee only. They sell no other products; they get no benefit from the advice they give. For independent advice that suits your situation, choose an independent, or fee only financial adviser. Do not rely on the following for **independent** financial advice:

- Stock brokers
- Insurance agents
- Mutual fund representatives
- Bankers
- Lawyers
- Others who may gain from advice to you

If for personal or other reasons you must work with one of the above groups, **agree beforehand that** whatever the outcome, you will not buy any of their products.

Independent financial advisers charge either a fixed fee for a consultation or consultations, or a fixed amount per hour. They give advice according to their abilities and without potential conflicts of interest. They target different markets; some set minimum net worth values for their clientele.

What Does She Do?

What can an independent financial adviser do for you? Many folks think of financial advisers primarily for investment advice. To be sure, they can help with this type of advice. However, you need to see a financial adviser even before you can afford to invest! I mentioned earlier the many financial choices available to the average person. In several chapters of this book, I indicated how I thought an independent adviser could help you. Specifically, after you establish your **Life Goals,** consult an independent financial adviser to prepare your net worth statement (the "still photograph" of your financial affairs at a specific date) and your financial plan.

Here are some examples of how an independent financial adviser can help you:

- Preparing a financial plan and a budget
- Preparing a cash flow statement
- Preparing a net worth statement
- Assisting to prepare a will—establishing trusts
- Tax planning—advice on RRSPs, RESPs, QSSPs,[2] and other aspects

- Retirement planning
- Investment advice
- General financial advice
- Insurance matters

Generally, they do not benefit from their recommendations.

For Whom Does She Work?

Before you work with a financial adviser, interview her to ensure she has the qualities to perform as you expect. Remember, she works for you; thus, you make decisions. After you receive advice, implement my three-step plan:

- First, ask clarifying questions!
- Second, ask further clarifying questions!
- Third, ask further clarifying questions until you understand the proposals!

Define and communicate your goals and values clearly and unequivocally. Your independent financial adviser should know that you are a Christian. If she is not a Christian, she must know specifically the values that guide you. For example, she should know that you do not tolerate anything but transparency on your tax returns; that you will pay all taxes due while taking advantage of available benefits.

Some technically acceptable and feasible financial decisions I reject because of my Christian beliefs. Although I know of the so-called benefits of financial leverage,[3] I do not apply leverage as the get-rich-quick industry recommends. I have many problems with their advice on leverage, but one is relevant! It violates the **GAS** principle: It's God's money. Thou shalt not speculate! Period!

Here are some questions to ask before you agree to work with an independent financial adviser:

- Is she independent?
- Does she represent any mutual funds, insurance, or other companies?
- What is her qualification and experience?
- Does she have references that you may check?
- How will she be compensated?
- Is she interested in taking you as a client?
- Will she have time for your account?

There are no enforceable national standards for financial advisers. Nevertheless, shop around before you make the final choice.

Think About This

Dig a well before you get thirsty.[4]

Chapter Notes:

[1] A share option is the time-limited right to buy shares in a company at a predetermined price. Company X may grant an option to you to buy 100 shares at $5 per share. Usually there is a waiting period before you may "exercise" the options. If in one year the shares were traded at $10 per share, you could exercise the option by purchasing those

shares at $5 then selling them. Alternatively, you may purchase shares and retain them.

2 Quebec Stock Savings Plan—A Provincial Government plan designed to encourage investment in Quebec companies. Naturally, there are restrictions on the qualifying amount, duration of savings, and so on.

3 Leverage is using other people's money to invest to create wealth for "me." The get-rich-quick industry preaches this!

4 Bob Phillips, *Phillips' Book of Great Thoughts and Funny Sayings* (Wheaton, IL: Tyndale House Publishers, Inc., 1993) p. 244.

16

A Forever to Remember

Reminiscing

It's 2:30 a.m., and for the past hour, I have been tossing and turning in bed. Since insomnia is one side-effect of Lariam,[1] I have decided to work on this book for a while.

After travelling for about twenty hours, at 1:00 a.m. I arrived in my hotel in Delhi, India, on the first leg of a two-week business trip. Like this trip, writing this book has been a long journey, but I am excited now! I have started to write the final chapter! It signals that shortly I will reach a major landmark on this project that began ten years ago with counselling Bill and Keisha. I never thought those sessions would become the base for a seminar and a book!

Reaching this milestone in a hotel room seems appropriate since I prepared for my seminars, my counselling sessions, and wrote most of this book on trans-Pacific business trips: at airports, on trains, on airplanes, and in hotel rooms.

A Brief Recap

The main message of the book is clear: God owns everything. The subsidiary purpose is obvious too: We must manage God's money knowing that we will account to Him for our actions. Accordingly, we must adhere rigorously to the **Gas** principle, which I will repeat here:

The GAS Principle

Key Truth #1: God Owns Everything (Psalm 24:1, Colossians 1:16)

Key Truth #2: Accept What You Have (1 Timothy 6:7-8, Hebrews 13:5)

Key Truth #3: Seek First His Kingdom and Submit Your Requests to Him (Matthew 6:33, Proverbs 19:21)

Once the **GAS principle** becomes ingrained and instinctive, we will be able to say with confidence:

The

Shepherd

gives

Gas

for
PEACE
on the
PLANE

The **PEACE** Budgetary Control system allows you to achieve **goals** systematically and is vital for managing God's money effectively. Follow it rigorously, always within the confines of the **Gas** principle, and He will bless you and you will eliminate money-related stress! It never stops!

Figure 1: The PEACE Budgetary Control System

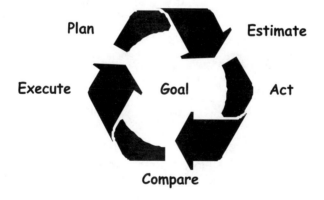

Plan · Estimate · Execute · Goal · Act · Compare

An Invitation

Managing money is merely one aspect of life, which cannot be isolated from others. How we spend money helps to define who we are! Hence, I invite you to think about **a forever that you will remember.**

Jesus told the eminent Jewish teacher Nicodemus that he needed a spiritual rebirth to gain eternal life.[2] Likewise, He told His disciples, "....unless you change and become like children, you will never enter the kingdom of heaven."[3] I ask you to utilize the faith, sincerity, and humility that a child displays to her parents to accept Jesus' invitation for this **forever to remember**.

This will be your pivotal lifetime decision; it is easy, yet profound. As a prelude to deciding, acknowledge the following:

- Jesus Christ lived on earth, died, then rose from the dead.
- He is the only true and living God.
- The Bible is the inspired Word of God and is infallible.
- You are a sinner, and you seek forgiveness.

Then from your heart, go for it!

- Decide to turn away from your sins.
- Ask Jesus to forgive your sins.
- Ask Him to take control of your life.

When you accept Christ into your life, your worldview changes as the Holy Spirit works within you. You may not become rich and famous, but you will gain direct access to our perfect Heavenly Father. Speak to Him! Listen to Him through His Word, the Bible! Start to attend a Bible-believing church! Meet with other believers for fellowship! Remember, His Word says that He will never leave you or forsake you.[4]

A Memorable Encounter

I will end with a slightly modified version of a story that I wrote in 1998 while waiting in the Qantas Lounge at Brisbane (Australia) airport:

Three individuals were walking along a deserted road one day. It was a gorgeous day! The sky was clear. The sun shone with an intensity that made a trip to the beach rather enticing. Several years later, as the boy reflected on this day, he marvelled at the circumstances that brought them together.

He had left school earlier than usual on his bike. He planned to take a short-cut through the park to hang out with his pals, but his bike got a flat tire.

The wealthy man was eccentric. He was going downtown via his usual route to avoid traffic when his car engine sputtered and his car stopped by the park. He had forgotten to fill up at the gas station that morning!

The doctor was walking toward the bus station. As usual, he would take the bus to the hospital where he worked as the Chief Surgeon.

Each of these persons lived in a different section of town. Miraculously, today their paths crossed at the southern and violent section of Victoria Park. The wealthy man lived in the most expensive neighbourhood in the North. The doctor lived in a poor, Southern area near the park. The sixteen-year-old lad lived on the main campus of the Liberal Arts University downtown with his dad, who was the caretaker.

As they walked together to the bus station, the boy said to the wealthy man,

"Sir, I go to school with your son. My friends say

that you and he live in a large home on that hill (the boy pointed Northward). They say it has every imaginable gadget! Yesterday I overheard your son mention that you take long vacations on your yacht. Cool! I want to be like you when I grow up! Tell me, sir, how does it feel to be relaxing on a yacht? You must have a lot of fun! You have everything!"

The wealthy man rubbed his chin and stared straight ahead. The boy felt embarrassed because of the sad look on his face. After what seemed like one hour but really was just one minute, the man replied,

"Everything! Does anyone ever have everything? Try to understand this: When I am on the ocean under the beautiful sky, yes, I am peaceful. The sky is clear. The water is calm. The only sound I hear is the gentle tapping of the water on the side of the yacht. Usually I enjoy this atmosphere... but for a short while only.

Afterwards I feel empty. I have too much to drink. I watch the TV. I watch videos. I read. What else should a man do? I mean, there must be more to life than this? Truly, I do get bored and tense after a few days. However, I am thinking of getting a much larger vessel that will present a bigger challenge."

The boy was shocked. He thought, 'This man has everything and is bored! That's impossible!'

As he prepared to ask another question, the doctor, who did not seem interested in the discussion, spoke.

"Five years ago I had it all; at least, that's what I thought then. However, like this gentleman, I felt

empty. Life seemed futile. I considered seriously going to Thailand to become a Buddhist Monk. I wanted to get away from it all. Tell me, lad, when you get a new bicycle or roller blades or basketball shoes, you enjoy them, don't you? But do you enjoy them in the same way six months later?"

The doctor did not pause to allow the boy to reply, but continued,

"I delayed my trip to Thailand several times. I guess I became so confused that I started to doubt the potential benefits of going. Eventually, I decided to stay home.

A colleague at the hospital introduced me to Transcendental Meditation. There was something about it that bothered me! When they initiated me, I felt uncomfortable with the religious ritual that the instructor performed. I guess I knew what I did not like, but I didn't know what I liked. I was sure that I did not want to get caught up in religious rituals. I had paid my dues when I was your age and had to go to church and watch people perform.

I am sorry, I am rambling, but I will make my point shortly. I became severely depressed and suicidal, and one Saturday morning, about 2:00 a.m., I was watching TV and met a man who changed my life."

The wealthy man and the boy became confused. Nobody spoke for a few minutes as they walked, until the doctor resumed.

"The preacher on the TV said something simple that got my attention: He said, 'I invite all of you watching this morning to step forward and accept Jesus Christ as your Lord and Saviour. I want you to know that when you do, you will start a personal relationship with Christ. I repeat, you will not be joining a religion, with a set of man-made rules; you will begin a personal relationship.'

The proverbial penny dropped that night! I had problems with church folks who seemed to behave one way on Sunday mornings and differently during the week. Now I understood from this preacher that Christianity is not about man-made rules but a relationship with Christ based on the unchanging principles in the Bible.

This man I met is no ordinary Man! Yes, Jesus Christ came to earth as a Man and was crucified, died, and rose again. Today, He is the only living God. This is the Man I met. I accepted Him as my Lord and Saviour that morning. You, too, can know this Man.

In the Bible, Jesus said that He is the good shepherd and we who believe in Him are His sheep. He said in the book of John (10:27-30) (RSV), 'My sheep hear my voice, and I know them, and they follow me; and I give them eternal life, and they shall never perish, and no one shall snatch them out of my hand. My Father, who has given them to me, is greater than all, and no one is able to snatch them out of the Father's hand. I and the Father are one.'"

Sombrely, the wealthy man said:

"May I collect you after work to learn more about your Man? Meanwhile, I must reflect on today's events."

At 11:30 p.m. that night, two cars pulled up along-side St. Mary's hospital, one with a wealthy man and his son, the other with a caretaker and his son. Patiently and silently, they waited to meet the doctor and His special Man.

Are you in one of those cars?[5]

Think About This

The God of Glory shine His mercy on you,
The God of Mercy shine His glory on you,
The god of this time is not the god
*   with whom you must commune,*
The god of this world is the evil,
*   against which you must become immune,*
Know the One who has been revealed to you
*   by His gracious majesty.*[6]

Chapter Notes:

[1] Lariam is the anti-malaria pill I take before, during, and after visiting certain countries. Insomnia is one of several side-effects.

[2] John 3:1-21

[3] Matthew 18:3

[4] Hebrews 13:5

[5] Michel A. Bell, "A Memorable Encounter" (Copyright © 1998, Michel A. Bell).

[6] Michel A. Bell, Excerpts from poem, "The God of Glory" (Copyright © 1998, Michel A. Bell).

Appendix 1: GAS Money Management System

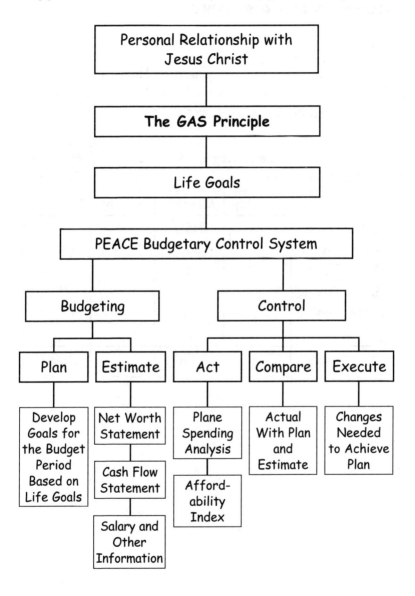

Appendix 2: PEACE Budget Computation Form: Income

Goals:

1. Accumulate Down Payment on Home in 3 Years
2. Balanced Budget Every Year
3. Vacation to Israel Next Year

Budget Categories	Frequency of Income/ Expenses			Monthly Budget
	Weekly	Monthly	Yearly	
Salary		3150		3150
Less: Giving		(315)		(315)
Less: Taxes		(735)		(735)
Less: Savings		(150)		(150)
Less: Capital Fund		(150)		(150)
Net Salary		1800		1800

Appendix 2: PEACE Budget Computation Form: Expenses

Budget Categories	Frequency of Income/ Expenses			Monthly Budget
	Weekly	Monthly	Yearly	
Rent		500		500
Car Expenses				
Loan Repay		300		300
Gasoline	15			60
Maintenance			360	30
Groceries	100			400
Entertainment & Recreation				
Meals	50			200
Video Rental	20			80
Movies	10			40
Telephone		50		50
Clothing			480	40
Gifts				
Birthdays			60	5
Christmas			120	10
Contingency	21			85
Total Expenses	216	850	1020	1800

Appendix 3-1: PEACE Budget Worksheet

PEACE Budget Worksheet

Date 98/9	Description	Total	Rent	Car Loan	Gas	Car Mtce	Groceries	Meals	Video	Movies	Telephone	Clothing	B'days	Christmas	Contingency
Sept 1	Allocation for Sept '98	1800	500	300	60	30	400	200	80	40	50	40	5	10	85
	Rent	500	500												
Sept 4	Lunch	35						35							
Sept 7	Balance left	1265	0	300	60	30	400	165	80	40	50	40	5	10	85
	Provigo	179					179								
Sept 9	Balance left	1086	0	300	60	30	221	165	80	40	50	40	5	10	85
	Cinema/Telephone	30								15	15				
Sept 11	Balance left	1056	0	300	60	30	221	165	80	25	35	40	5	10	85
	Shell	25			25										
Sept 13	Balance left	1031	0	300	35	30	221	165	80	25	35	40	5	10	85
	Royal Bank	300		300											
Sept 15	Balance left	731	0	0	35	30	221	165	80	25	35	40	5	10	85
	Dinner	75						75							
Sept 17	Balance left	656	0	0	35	30	221	90	80	25	35	40	5	10	85
	Provigo	150					150								
Sept 21	Balance left	506	0	0	35	30	71	90	80	25	35	40	5	10	85
	Shell	15			15										
Sept 23	Balance left	491	0	0	20	30	71	90	80	25	35	40	5	10	85
	Video	30							30						
Sept 23	Balance left	461	0	0	20	30	71	90	50	25	35	40	5	10	85
	Provigo	100					100								
Sept 27	Balance left	361	0	0	20	30	-29	90	50	25	35	40	5	10	85
	Sears	76										76			
Sept 29	Balance left	285	0	0	20	30	-29	90	50	25	35	-36	5	10	85
	Telephone	30									30				
Sept 30	Balance left	255	0	0	20	30	-29	90	50	25	5	-36	5	10	85
	Budget For October 1998	**1800**	**500**	**300**	**60**	**30**	**400**	**200**	**80**	**40**	**50**	**40**	**5**	**10**	**85**
	Total Allocation Oct	2055	500	300	80	60	371	290	130	65	55	4	10	20	170

Appendix 3-2: Weekly Budget Worksheet

Yearly Budget	PEACE Budget Worksheet — Budget Item	Actual Expenses for Month				Actual for Month	Monthly Budget
		Week	Week	Week	Week		
	Income:						
	Bank Balance per Cheque book						
	Income – Regular						
	– Interest						
	– Other						
	Total Income						
	Expenses:						
	Tithing						
	Savings						
	Capital Fund						
	Household expenses						
	Groceries						
	Toiletries						
	Telephone						
	Gifts						
	Clothing						
	Emergency						
	Total Expenses						
	Excess income over expenses						
	Notes:						

Appendix 3-3: PEACE Budget Worksheet

PEACE Budgetary Control System

	December 1st to 15th		December 16th to 31st		Christmas Expenses	
	Budget (1st to 15th)	Actual (1st to 15th)	Budget (16th to 31st)	Actual (16th to 31st)	Budget	Act
Month of ___			**Month ___**			
Income:			Income:		Income	
Salary			Salary			
Expenses			Expenses		Expenses	
Tithe			Tithe		Clothes	
Savings			Savings		Gifts	
Capital Fund			Capital Fund			
Mortgage			Mortgage			
Loan repayment			Loan repayment			
			Insurance			
Groceries			Groceries			
Sub-Total			Sub-Total			
Gas			Gas			
Sub-Total			Sub-Total			
Phone			Phone			
Cable			Hydro			
Christmas			Christmas			
Sub-Total			Sub-Total			
Video			Vacation			
			Snack			
Total Expenses			Total Expenses		0	
Excess Income/(Expenses)	0	0	Excess Income/(Expenses)	0	0	

Appendix 3-4: Weekly Budget Worksheet

PEACE Budget Worksheet

"Ah Lord God you have made the heavens and the earth by your great power and by your outstretched arms, nothing is too difficult for you." Jeremiah 32:17

This "weekly summary section" shows balance left each week for each category and for the total budget

(A) Budget Category	(B) Date	(C) Description	(D) Spent $	(E) Budget Left	(F) Month of — Comments on "Spent" col "D"	(G)	(H)	(I)	(J)
		SECTION 1				Weekly Summary - SECTION 2			
						Budget Allocation Left: Week Ending			
						/	/	/	/
BUDGET LEFT * up to PRIOR Month $	/	ALLOCATION FOR MONTH * from Column "A"							
Budget for current Month $	/								
Allocation$	/								
	/								
	/								
Total SPENT for MONTH =>		Total budget left each week =>	$						
BUDGET LEFT * up to PRIOR Month $	/	ALLOCATION FOR MONTH * from Column "A"							
Budget for current Month $	/								
Allocation $	/								
	/								
	/								
Total SPENT for MONTH =>		Total budget left each week =>	$						
BUDGET LEFT * up to PRIOR Month $	/	ALLOCATION FOR MONTH * from Column "A"							
Budget for current Month $	/								
Allocation $	/								
	/								
	/								
Total SPENT for MONTH =>		Total budget left each week =>	$						
Total spent this page =>		Total this page =>> Total all pages =>>	$			0			

* "Allocation for month" includes the current month's budget plus or minus the "budget left" from the start of the period to the prior month from Section 2.

"I am the Lord the God of all mankind. Is anything too hard for me?" Jeremiah 32:27

Appendix 4: House Purchase Guide

Goals				
Reason For Buying The House				
Key Criteria				
Location				
Size of house (sq.ft)				
Number of Bedrooms				
Other				
House Selection Guide	House #1	House #2	House #3	House #4
Address				
General External Appearance				
Roof				
Yard				
Other				
Entrance Hall				
Ceiling				
Floor				
Other				
Living Room				
Ceiling				
Floor				
Fixtures				
Drapes				
Other				
Kitchen				
Ceiling				
Floor				
Fixtures				
Drapes				
Other				
Den				
Ceiling				
Floor				
Fixtures				
Drapes				
Other				
Bedroom - Master				
Ceiling				
Floor				
Fixtures				
Drapes				
Other				
Bedroom - #2				
Ceiling				
Floor				
Fixtures				
Drapes				
Other				
Bedroom # 3				
Ceiling				
Floor				
Fixtures				
Drapes				
Other				
Fireplace/Basement				
Garage/Swimming pool				
Taxes				
Access to Amenities/Facilities				
Commuting Facilities				
Medical facilities				
Shopping facilities				
Other				
Possession date				
Estimated repairs necessary				
Rating:Scale of 1(Bad) to 10 (Best)				
General Comments				

Glossary

Affordability Index: A quantification of answers to the five questions of the PLANE spending analysis that helps you to decide whether or not to commit to any major expenditure.

Amortization Period: The period over which you repay your entire mortgage.

Asset: Things of value that you own.

Bankruptcy: It occurs when a borrower can no longer pay what he owes and his lenders are unwilling to restructure his loans or provide more credit.

Bond: A loan (typically for longer than ten years) where the borrower promises to pay the lender a specified interest per year or when the loan is repaid in full.

Budget Deficit: Expenses exceeding income during the budget period.

Budget: A record of the results of the **planning and estimating** processes.

Budgeting: Systematic planning, estimating, allocating, and recording of resources to attain your goal or set of goals; counting the cost as in Luke 14:28.

Capital Fund: An account maintained to finance major purchases and large maintenance expenses to eliminate crises from annual budgets and to enable planning and scheduling of necessary major maintenance and major purchases.

Cash Flow: Cash inflows and cash outflows during a specific period.

Common Stock (Stock): A document that represents ownership in a company.

Compound Interest: Interest paid or received on accumulated interest earned during previous periods, in addition to the amount loaned or deposited.

Consumer Price Index (CPI): A CPI is a means to measure the total change in the prices of retail goods and services that we buy. The measurement is done over a specific period (one month), and for a precise basket of goods and services.

Debt Repayment Ratio: Total loan payments (including mortgage principal and interest) for the period (one year) as a percentage of gross income for the period.

Discounting (Discounted): The process of finding the present value of a series of future cash flows.

Discretionary Expense: An expense that you may decide not to incur such as entertainment and a vacation.

Disposable Income: The income you have available after taxes and payroll deductions have been taken from your salary.

Equity: Assets minus liabilities (same as net worth).

Estimate: The likely cost of the **plan**—the cost of the steps in the **plans**.

Future Value: The value of money in the future; it is influenced by interest.

GAS Principle: Three Key Truths in the Bible concerning money:

- **Key Truth #1: God Owns Everything** (Psalm 24:1, Colossians 1:16)
- **Key Truth #2: Accept What You Have** (1 Timothy 6:7-8, Hebrews 13:5)
- **Key Truth #3: Seek First His Kingdom and Submit Your Requests to Him** (Matthew 6:33, Proverbs 19:21)

Goal: Your **destination**—where you wish to go.

Inflation: A sustained and general rise in prices.

Lease: A rental agreement where someone (the lessee) agrees to use an asset and pays a fee to the owner (the lessor).

Lessee: Person receiving the asset from the lessor.

Lessor: Person granting the lease of an asset he owns to someone else, the lessee.

Leverage: Using borrowed funds usually to acquire an asset.

Line of Credit: A short-term, revolving loan that banks extend to certain customers based on a minimum net worth and favourable credit rating.

Marginal Tax Rate: The tax rate that applies to the last dollar of income that you earn.

Maximum Debt Ratio: Total of all loans on the net worth statement as a percentage of the total liabilities side of the net worth statement.

Mortgage Term: The life of the mortgage loan agreement with the financial institution.

Mortgage: A loan with a designated property (your home) as security.

Mortgage Open: With an **open** mortgage, you can repay the principal fully or partially anytime without a penalty.

Mortgage Closed: For a **closed** mortgage, you pay a penalty if you repay before the term expires.

Mortgage—Fixed Rate: A mortgage with fixed payments and the interest rate does not change during the mortgage term. Table IX shows the impact of a fixed rate mortgage.

Mortgage—Variable Rate: A mortgage with fixed payments, but which allows for fluctuation in interest rates due to changing market conditions. Changes in the interest rate will determine how much of each payment will go toward the principal. Thus, if the mortgage interest rate increases, the allocation to principal as in Table IX will decrease and vice versa.

Mutual Fund: A Mutual Fund is an organization that invests pooled funds of many depositors. Usually a professional manager manages it. Mutual Funds tend to specialize, each with a different investment objective.

Net Present Value: The present value of future cash flows discounted at a specific interest rate, minus an initial outlay.

Net Worth Statement: A statement showing assets, liabilities, and equity.

Net Worth: Assets minus liabilities.

PEACE Budgetary Control System: A system that allows you to achieve **goals** systematically in the following manner:

- **PLAN** for a specific period to accomplish precise **goals**.
- **ESTIMATE** and record the expenses needed to achieve those **goals**.
- **ACT** on the **plan and record** actual results as you progress toward your **goals**.
- **COMPARE actual** results **with** the **plan** and with the **estimated expenses** required to attain the **goals**.
- **EXECUTE** changes necessary to remain on course to realize the **goals**.

PLANE Spending Analysis: Five questions to answer before you commit to any major expenditure:

P   Did I **Plan** this expenditure and did I include it in my budget?

L   Will the expenditure increase my **Loans**?

A   Are there realistic **Alternatives** to achieve my spending objective?

N   Is the expenditure **Necessary** to achieve my spending objective?

E   Is this the most **Effective** use of resources now, relative to my **Life Goals and budget goals**?

Plan: Your **journey**—the steps to achieve your **goal**.

Present Value: The value of money today.

Real Interest Rate: Actual interest rate less inflation rate.

Registered Education Savings Plan (RESP): A vehicle to help you to save toward your children's (or other identified beneficiary of the plan) post-secondary education. Unlike an RRSP, you do not get a tax deduction for the amounts you contribute to the RESP, but the income on the amounts saved is compounded and not taxed until withdrawn.

Registered Retirement Savings Plan (RRSP): A savings plan to which your annual contribution is tax deductible. Since 1990, the maximum annual allowable tax deduction is 18% of your earned income for the prior year (to a maximum amount) less benefits accrued under your registered pension plans and deferred profit sharing plans for the previous year.

Tax Shield: The tax deduction you gain from expenditures.

Trust: Property held by one party (the trustee) for the benefit of another (the beneficiary).

About the Author

Michel A. Bell (Mike) has been married to Doreen Bell for over 30 years. They have four adult children: Bill Matheuszik (son-in-law) is married to Keisha, and Shabbir who is married to Lesley Ann (daughter-in-law), and three grand children: Adrienne, Jesse and Dylan. They are Jamaican-born Canadians living in Baie d'Urfe, Quebec.

The couple has lived in five countries including Japan, the United Kingdom, and the USA. Michel (Mike) has held many senior finance positions in the ALCAN Inc., Montreal, Quebec group, including Regional Vice President Finance and Legal for Alcan's Pacific subsidiary, and Chief Financial Officer for Alcan's worldwide Alumina and Chemicals businesses. Currently, Mike is Director of Business Planning for the world-wide bauxite, alumina and specialty chemicals group.

He holds a Master's degree in Management Science from the Sloan School of Management at Massachusetts Institute of Technology (M.I.T) and is a Chartered Certified Accountant (UK).

Encouraged by his children, over ten years ago, Mike started presenting basic money management concepts and principles to individuals, couples, and groups.

ORDER FORM

To order *Managing God's Money—The Basics* **or** *Managing God's Money—The Basics Workbook*, please use the order form below (please print):

Name: _____

Address: _____

City: _____ State/Prov: _____

Zip/Postal Code: _____ Telephone: _____

____copies of the book @ $14.95 Cdn / $10.95 US: $_____

___copies of the workbook @ $14.95 Cdn / $10.95 US: $_____

Shipping: ($3.00 first book – $1.00 each add. book) $_____

Total amount enclosed: **$_____**

PAYABLE BY ☐ Check ☐ Money Order
☐ Mastercard ☐ VISA

Name on Card _____

Card Number _____ Exp. ___/___

Signature on Card _____

Send to: *Essence Publishing*
44 Moira St. West, Belleville, ON K8P 1S3
Phone: 1-800-238-6376
E-mail: info@essencegroup.com
Internet: www.essencegroup.com

For more information on **Managing God's Money Ministres**, visit ***www.managinggodsmoney.com***